HAVE YOU EVER DRIVEN PAST A FACTOR... THERE BECAUSE THEY LOOK LIKE MISER... (AND BURPS!). EVEN IF YOU CAN'T SEE THE AWFUL PLACE F... ROAD (AND YOU USUALLY CAN'T--THEY HIDE THESE THINGS FROM SIGHT FOR A REASON), YOU CAN CATCH A BIG WHIFF OF THE FECAL STENCH FROM A GREAT DISTANCE. THAT'S NOT GOOD, BECAUSE THOSE ANIMAL FARTS ARE PART OF THE ONETHIRD OF THE WORLD'S METHANE GAS THAT'S PRODUCED BY LIVESTOCK. METHANE HAS A GLOBAL WARMING POWER 86 TIMES THAT OF CO2. NOT ONLY THAT, LIVESTOCK IS RESPONSIBLE FOR 65PERCENT OF ALL EMISSIONS OF NITROUS OXIDE; A GREENHOUSE GAS 296 TIMES MORE DESTRUCTIVE THAN CARBON DIOXIDE AND WHICH STAYS IN THE ATMOSPHERE FOR 150 YEARS. NOT GOOD.

AND IT GETS WORSE. ACCORDING TO THE UNITED NATIONS FOOD AND AGRICULTURE ORGANIZATION (FAO), RAISING ANIMALS FOR FOOD IS RESPONSIBLE FOR 7.1 GIGATONNES OF CO2 EQUIVALENT EMISSION PER YEAR, OR 14.5% OF GLOBAL EMISSIONS (1). THAT'S RIGHT, YOUR HAMBURGER ADDICTION IS SLOWLY CHOKING MOTHER EARTH. ANIMAL AGRICULTURE PRODUCES MORE GREENHOUSE GAS EMISSIONS THAN ALL THE EMISSIONS FROM THE ENTIRE EARTH'S VEHICLES COMBINED. THAT IS CORRECT, COMBINED. READ THAT AGAIN BECAUSE I HAD TO . WE'RE BASICALLY LIVING IN A HORROR FILM BUT UNLIKE THE DUMMIES AT THE MOVIES, WE HAVE THE CHANCE TO CHOOSE NOT TO GO BACK IN THE HOUSE WITH BLOOD SEEPING FROM ITS WALLS. I'D SAY THAT'S A GOOD CALL! BY CUTTING ANIMALS AND ANIMAL PRODUCTS OUT OF YOUR DIET, YOU HELP REDUCE 51% OF THE WORLD'S GREENHOUSE GAS EMISSIONS PRODUCED EVERY YEAR (3). EXCITING STUFF! YOU ARE BASICALLY A SUPERHERO WHO USES A KNIFE AND FORK TO SAVE THE WORLD, WHICH IS WAY COOLER THAN A CAPE. (I THINK. YOU CAN USE BOTH, IF YOU WANT; A PERSON IN A CAPE HOLDING A KNIFE AND FORK IS PRETTY MUCH THE COOLEST CAT ALIVE.)

DAY 2
WATER CONSUMPTION

GOOD NEWS, EVERYBODY! IF YOU AREN'T ALREADY IN THE CORNER ROCKING BACK AND

FORTH IN THE FETAL POSITION OVER HOW WE'RE ALL SCREWED AFTER THE LAST CHAPTER,

I'M HERE TO PUSH YOU OVER THE EDGE. NOT ONLY IS OUR SLOVENLY DEVOTION TO MEAT A

DAIRY COMPLETELY CHANGING OUR CLIMATE, IT'S ALSO SUCKING UP OUR WATER SUPPLY.

IT'S A TWOFER! LUCKY US! (OR REALLY, REALLY NOT.) YOU KNOW HOW YOU STOPPED

SHOWERING SO OFTEN BECAUSE OF THE DROUGHT AND NOW YOU SMELL LIKE A SUNBAKE

COACHELLA PORTA POTTY? WELL, YOUR STINKY BUTT WAS ALL FOR NOTHING BECAUSE, AS

TURNS OUT, ONLY FIVE PERCENT OF U.S. WATER IS CONSUMED BY PRIVATE HOMES. (1) YE

FIVE PERCENT. THAT'S IT. ALL OF THE SHOWERING IN THE WORLD ISN'T GOING TO USE UP

ALL THAT WATER SO PLEASE, HERE'S A TOWEL, COME BACK WHEN YOU SMELL HUMAN

AGAIN.

WELCOME BACK! NOW, YOU MIGHT BE WONDERING WHERE ALL THAT WATER IS GOING IF

YOU'RE NOT SINGLE HANDEDLY SAVING CALIFORNIA WITH YOUR FRENCH BATHS. WELL,

HERE'S THE WACK TRUTH: CALIFORNIA EXPORTS 100 BILLION GALLONS OF WATER IN THE

FORM OF ALFALFA EVERY YEAR TO ASIA FOR MEAT AND DAIRY PRODUCTION (2)!

EVEN BIGGER PICTURE: GROWING FOOD FOR LIVESTOCK CONSUMES 55%

OF WATER IN THE UNITED STATES (3). THAT'S OVER HALF OF

OUR WATER GOING TO RAISING ANIMALS WHO ARE DESTINED TO BE

SLAUGHTERED SO SOMEONE CAN EAT A BIG MAC THAT'S BEEN

SWEATING UNDER A HEAT LAMP ALL DAY. YUM!

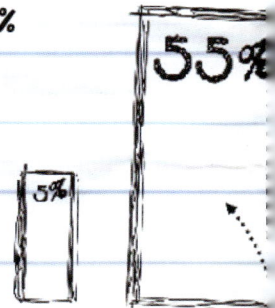

5% of water in the U.S. is used for domestic purposes, whereas 55% is used for animal agriculture

You see, we're not just hurting cows and pigs and chickens and goats with our lust for dead animals and their secretions, nope. We're also hurting every other animal on earth, considering that animal agriculture is the leading driver of species extinction. (1) Our insatiable desire for baconwrapped hot dogs is destroying other wildlife, their habitat, and their water sources. In addition to all that awfulness, more than 175 threatened or endangered species are imperiled by livestock on federal lands. (2) And it doesn't just end there — grazing livestock destroys natural vegetation and damages wildlife habitats, destroys water ways and causes wild fires. Perhaps you need some more specifics of different species/animals that are on the brink of extinction? Maybe Smokey the Bear should've instead stomped out a few fast food restaurants to help prevent forest fires? Maybe it's not too late? Make it happen, cartoon bear!

So even if you couldn't care less about pigs, maybe you care about the wildlife species indigenous to your area and the fact that future generations will never get to know the beauty that is gazing into a grazing elk's giant soulful eyes.
(And adorable animal YouTube videos, while honestly wonderful, will never be as magical as the real thing.)

DAY 4

ENVIRONMENTAL IMPACT OF DAIRY

PLEASE PUT DOWN YOUR LARGE GLASS OF CHILLED COW'S MUCUS (AKA, MILK) IF YOU DON'T WANT TO BARF THAT GOOPY GARBAGE ALL OVER YOUR LAPTOP. OK, NOW THAT YOU'RE FULLY PREPARED TO DEAL WITH THE FOLLOWING MESSAGE OF FUNK, HERE'S ONE OF THE GROSSEST FACTS OF ALL TIME:
EVERY MINUTE OF EVERYDAY, SEVEN MILLION POUNDS OF EXCREMENT ARE PRODUCED BY ANIMALS RAISED FOR FOOD IN THE UNITED STATES...
IS YOUR JAW ON THE GROUND? AND ARE YOU IMAGINING ME SHOVELING ANIMAL POOP IN YOUR GAPING MAW? BECAUSE YOU SHOULD BE. THAT'S HOW DISTURBED YOU SHOULD BE BY THIS VERY DISTURBING FACT.

SO, WHILE MUCH OF THE UNITED STATES GRAPPLES WITH EVER DWINDLING RESERVOIRS, THE NUMBER ONE REASON FOR OUR LACK OF H2O OFTEN GOES UNADDRESSED. AMERICANS WOULD RATHER NOT WASH THEIR CARS FOR MONTHS THAN FORGO A VISIT TO THE HEART ATTACK GRILL. (WHICH IS A REAL RESTAURANT THAT EXISTS AND HAS LITERALLY KILLED SEVERAL PEOPLE DURING, OR IMMEDIATELY AFTER, THEIR MEAL.) YOU SEE, IT TAKES 2,500 GALLONS OF WATER TO PRODUCE JUST ONE POUND OF BEEF (4) AND IF YOU SKIP A HAMBURGER, YOU SAVE 660 GALLONS OF WATER (5) - THE EQUIVALENT OF TWO MONTHS OF SHOWERS. BY JUST REPLACING YOUR DEAD COW PATTY WITH A VEGGIE BURGER, SO, YOU CAN SMELL DECENT AND SAVE THE EARTH. ISN'T LIFE EASY AND FUN? (DON'T ANSWER THAT.) AND IT'S NOT JUST BEEF THAT'S SUCKING US DRY, PLENTY OF ANIMAL BYPRODUCTS ARE JUST AS THIRSTY. WRAP YOUR BRAIN AROUND THE FACT THAT IT TAKES 477 GALLONS OF WATER TO PRODUCE ONE POUND OF EGGS, 900 GALLONS TO CREATE A POUND OF CHEESE (6), AND A WHOPPING 1,000 GALLONS TO MAKE ONE GALLON OF MILK (7). YES, IT TAKES 1,000 GALLONS OF WATER TO MAKE ONE MEASLY GALLON OF MILK. I'M SORRY BUT I WILL NEVER STOP SHAKING MY HEAD AT THAT FACT. ALL OF OUR WATER IS GOING TO CREATING GARBAGE FOOD MADE OF SUFFERING AND CHEMICALS, YET WE THINK WE'RE MAKING A DENT BY TURNING OFF THE WATER WHEN WE BRUSH OUR TEETH? IT'S TIME TO WAKE UP AND SMELL THE PARCHED EARTH REALITY (SMELLS KINDA LIKE MANURE ON FIRE). WE'RE NEVER GONNA BE SERIOUS ABOUT WATER CONSERVATION UNTIL WE START EXAMINING OUR FOOD CHOICES.

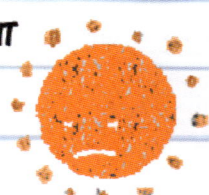

IT TAKES 2,500 GALLONS OF WATER TO PRODUCE JUST 1 POUND OF BEEF!!!

GROWING FOOD FOR LIVESTOCK CONSUMES 56% OF WATER IN THE UNITED STATES

DAY 3 SPECIES EXTINCTION

Do you love watching California Grizzly Bears frolic with their young in a field of wild flowers? Do you think Mexican Grey Wolves are the coolest creatures on Earth? Do you enjoy watching prairie dogs play whackamole in the wild? Well then you better bookmark some YouTube videos of "adorable animals being adorable" because if we keep doing what we're doing, that's all that's gonna be left. You might say you don't care about the climate or the water supply, so you probably see no need to abstain from chomping into a juicy burger and washing it down with chunky beef stew? Well, perhaps some cuddly wuddly panda bears could help persuade you into giving a crap?

LIVESTOCK COVERS 45% OF THE EARTH'S TOTAL LAND

And that disgustingness isn't only bad news for the farmers who work "in the sh*t"— although it is very bad for them considering the illnesses associated with living and working around such copious amounts of feces (2) and the fact that sometimes farmers die horribly by choking on, or drowning in giant openair manure lagoons (3) —it's bad news for all of us. Chew on this fact (or don't): one large dairy operation with 2,500 dairy cows produces the same amount of waste as a city of 411,000 people. Where do you think all that poop is going? It's polluting our air, our land, and our water. The sheer amount of shit flooding our waterways is creating enormous ocean dead zones, where the oxygen is literally zapped from the water and everything dies.

The heavy metals, hormones, antibiotics and ammonia in the feces slide straight into the water we use for drinking, swimming and fishing. And when it gets into the air, there's a whole 'nother slew of problems including nausea and headaches. And after prolonged exposure, throat and eye irritation, respiratory illness, lung inflammation, and increased vulnerability to respiratory diseases such as asthma. It's all bad. It's all very, very bad. It is the opposite of whatever "all that and a bag of chips" is. ("Not all that and a bag of poop on fire in your face"?) (5) And the problem just extrapolates from there — as the feces migrate into the environment on a larger scale, it reduces agricultural yields and makes plants more vulnerable to disease. Basically, your need for a glass of cow's milk might mean the end of civilization. (I know, it's dramatic, but I feel the need for drama is here. Plus, I've been watching a lot of Project Runway so I'm ready to call people out!)

We have to ease up on our cow cheese consumption or we're all gonna be up shit's creek - literally (apologize on behalf of mysef and my entire family for that depressing fact and the even more depressing pun).

2,500 **DAIRY COWS PRODUCE THE SAME AMOUNT OF WASTE AS A CITY OF** 411,000 **PEOPLE!**

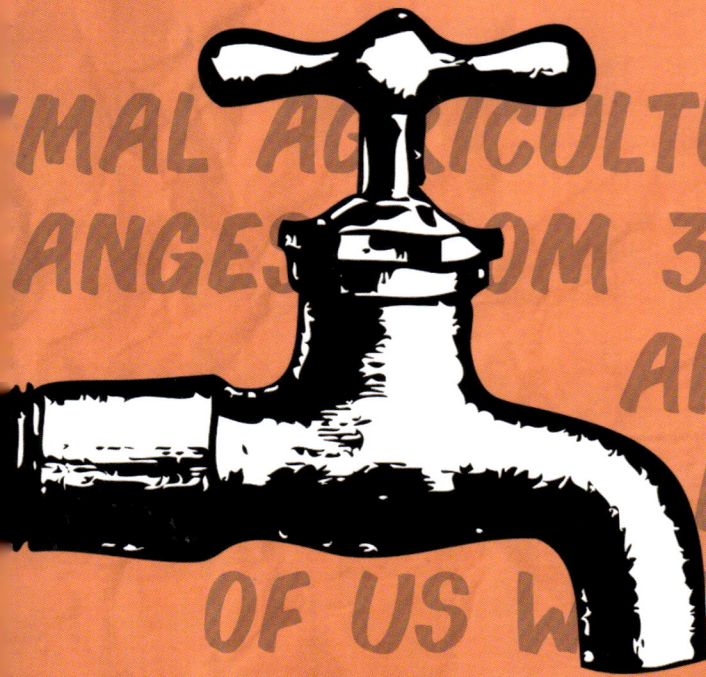

BECAUSE YOU ARE EXCELLENT AT READING AND ALSO VERY GOOD LOOKING, YOU ALREADY KNOW THAT PRIVATE HOME WATER USAGE IS A (LITERAL) DROP IN THE BUCKET COMPARED TO THE H2O USED FOR ANIMAL AGRICULTURE. IN CALIFORNIA, THE SUNSHINE STATE WHERE ALL THE GIRLS WEAR POLKA DOT BIKINIS, HOUSEHOLDS CONSUME LESS THAN FIVE PERCENT OF WATER WHILE MEAT AND DAIRY PRODUCTION SUCKS UP A WHOPPING 47 PERCENT. (1) TO BREAK IT DOWN EVEN FURTHER, A QUARTER-POUND BEEF BURGER IS THE EQUIVALENT OF TWO MONTHS OF SHOWERING! (2) TWO FREAKING MONTHS. IF YOU STOP EATING BURGERS, YOU CAN TAKE 17 SHOWERS A DAY AND BE THE SQUEAKY CLEANEST WEIRDO IN THE LAND AND NOBODY COULD SAY JACK TO YOU. EXCEPT MAYBE YOUR THERAPIST.

SO, COMPARED TO MEAT AND DAIRY, HOUSEHOLD USAGE AIN'T NOTHING. BUT WHAT ABOUT COMPARED TO OTHER ENVIRONMENTAL DISASTERS? WELL, LET'S TAKE FRACKING (HYDRAULIC FRACTURING) FOR EXAMPLE, WHICH USES 70,140 BILLION GALLONS OF WATER ANNUALLY. (3) NOW, COMPARE THAT TO ANIMAL AGRICULTURE, WHOSE CONSUMPTION RANGES FROM 3476 TRILLION GALLONS ANNUALLY. (4) WOW, SO COMPARED TO OTHER THINGS THAT ARE EVIL, ANIMAL AGRICULTURE IS MEGA EVIL. IT'S LIKE THE DEVIL IF THE DEVIL POPPED A BUNCH OF "EVIL NUTBAG" STEROIDS AND GREW TEN BILLION TIMES LARGER AND MORE DEVIL-LIKE. AM I GETTING MY POINT ACROSS? IT'S BAD. REALLY REALLY BAD. IF YOU'RE AGAINST THE DANGEROUS AND DESTRUCTIVE PROCESS OF DRILLING AND INJECTING FLUID INTO THE GROUND IN ORDER TO FRACTURE ROCKS TO RELEASE NATURAL GAS BECAUSE OF HOW MUCH WATER IT USES, THEN YOU HAVE TO BE EVEN MORE UPSET ABOUT ANIMAL AGRICULTURE. THAT'S JUST SCIENCE. AND BEING A DECENT PERSON.

OK, SO YOU GET IT. AND NOW YOU'RE THINKING BUT WHAT THE HAY AM I SUPPOSED TO EAT IF I CAN'T GOBBLE DOWN BACON CHEESY BLASTERS DRENCHED IN MAYONNAISE AND WHIPPED CREAM FOR EVERY MEAL? DO I REALLY HAVE TO EAT SHAFTS OF DRY WHEAT AND RIVER ROCK TO BE A REAL ENVIRONMENTALIST?! THE SHORT ANSWER IS NO AND THE LONG ANSWER IS, "HECK NO! REAL ENVIRONMENTALISTS EAT ALL THE GOOD FOOD; TRUST! WE'LL GET TO ALL THAT LATER ON, BUT SERIOUSLY: BUST OUT YOUR EATING PANTS. "IF WE REALLY WANT TO SEE THE DIFFERENCE IN WATER CONSUMPTION FOR FOODS, WE NEED TO LOOK AT SOME LEGIT INFORMATION. ACCORDING TO NATIONAL GEOGRAPHIC (VERY LEGIT), HERE'S HOW MANY GALLONS OF WATER IT TAKES TO PRODUCE A POUND OF THE FOLLOWING PRODUCTS (5): BEEF: 1,799 - WE SAY IN FILM 2,500 GALLONS, PROB NEED TO USE THAT SOURCE, AS GOES FOR THE REST OF THESE)

GOAT 1,799
SHEEP 731
PORK 576
CHICKEN 468
MILK 880
WINE 1,008
COFFEE 880
BARLEY 198
WHEAT 132
RICE 449
POTATOES 119
CORN 108
SOYBEAN 216
CHEESE 600
CHOCOLATE 3,170
SUGAR 198
QUANTITY: 1
APPLE 18
ORANGE 13
EGG 53
BURGER 660
SLICE OF BREAD 11

ANIMAL AGRICULTURE IS RESPONSIBLE FOR 20%-33% OF ALL FRESH WATER CONSUMPTION IN THE WORLD TODAY.

AND IT'S NOT JUST THE THINGS YOU EAT. FOR EXAMPLE, A HALF-POUND OF NASTY OL' DEAD COW SKIN (AKA LEATHER) USES 1,096 GALLONS, WHEREAS A COTTON T-SHIRT ONLY USES 713. IT'S JUST A WHOLE DIFFERENT BALL GAME! ONE THAT'S FILLED WITH FRUITS AND VEGGIES AND GRAINS AND AWESOMENESS! (TRUE FACT.)

DAY 6: WATER POLLUTION

This chapter is going to be about how unicorns are real and that one day you'll get to snuggle them in Heaven whilst sitting on a cloud made of marshmallows and baby giggles!

JK, it's about ocean dead zones. What's a dead zone? No, it doesn't involve a bunch of hippies living in trailers and eating their hemp bracelets for sustenance. (That's called a "Grateful Dead Zone") An ocean dead zone is an area where the oxygen concentration in the water is so low that animal life suffocates and dies. (1) Wanna guess the leading contributors to these dead zones (as well as fresh water pollution)? If you've been reading /sobbing along with me, you've probably guessed it: it's animal crap. (2) The excrement produced by livestock often makes its way into oceans, streams, creeks, rivers, lakes, aquifers and seas. Additionally, fertilizers, pesticides and herbicides run off the millions of acres of feed crop fields into local water. (3) The sheer magnitude of funk overwhelms properly functioning ecosystems and leads to hypertrophication, which causes species displacement, clogged waterways, and oxygen depletion (3). Or, in non-science nerd terms, because it's contaminated with Mountains of Crap, the water loses its oxygen and all sea life dies.

And that all adds up to some very funky H20. Or, to make it fancy for the science-minded amongst you who won't just take "animal agriculture is turning our water into antibiotic barf!" as a proven fact (even though it is; come at me, science!), what that means is that our current farming practices cause about 70 percent of the pollution in the nation's rivers and streams. (4)

And here's some more poop facts for you since they're apparently my specialty: In one year, animals produce 1.4 billion tons of waste in the US alone, 130 times more than the American population. That's about five tons of animal waste produced per one human. And let's not forget, these animals don't have toilets or functioning septic systems and so their shit is just out there, choking us all to death. This is not how I imagined dying! I wanted to go at age 279 surrounded by friends and loved ones who feed me churros until I drift off into that final sleep.

EWWWWWW!

As if people weren't shitty enough already. (Zing!) And a lot of that poop isn't just ending up in our food, air, and sewage systems—it's also finding its way into our water supply. Which is what we've been talking about all chapter. Basically, poop and water don't mix except when they really do and it's killing everything, capisce?

EVERY MINUTE
7 MILLION POUNDS OF EXCREMENT ARE PRODUCED BY ANIMALS RAISED FOR FOOD IN THE U.S.

ANIMAL AGRICULTURE IS THE LEADING CAUSE OF OCEAN DEAD ZONES

DAY 7 WILD LIFE

You know how animals are the greatest and you love them so much but whatever, cows are raised to be slaughtered and so it's fine. Well, first off, cows are smart, cool, unique sentient beings with as much personality (if not more) than your beloved pet, and also, even if you think it's A-OK to raise some animals to be murdered so people can eat garbage food that's killing them (fun fact!), you should know that by doing so, you're also contributing to the leading cause of wildlife being killed due to habitat loss. (1) The crappy salisbury steak dinner at your third cousin's wedding (that you didn't even want to go to! Damn you, societal expectations!) is killing off all sorts of gorgeous wild creatures, including elk, deer, pronghorn, Mexican gray wolves, and ridiculously majestic California Grizzly Bears. That's because cattle ranchers don't want to share land, water, and other resources with the animals who originally inhabited the land because they can't raise as many cows (to die) if they do. And don't get me started on how much some people love "grass-fed" cows because they're so much more environmentally friendly. Sorry, bub! It takes 10-50 acres to feed just one of those cows. It's total lunacy!

MORE WILD HORSES AND BURROS ARE IN GOVERNMENT HOLDING FACILITIES THAN ARE FREE ON THE RANGE.

***

(Reason why? The ranchers and cows don't want to, and can't share the land with any other animals due to limited water and food on these areas. And "grass fed" is ironically the biggest culprit, as it takes up to 10-50 acres for just ONE COW!?!) Not only that, if any of those animals don't leave their natural habitat to make room for massive feedlots, well then, they're just killed. Millions of taxpayer dollars are wasted on hazardous, ineffective, and frankly, terrifying, "predator control programs", which target wolves and coyotes for simply existing on land where they've lived for hundreds of years. (2)

Oh and don't you love horses? Yeah, you do. Admit it. You wanted a pony when you were a kid and you pretty much still do because they are the most ridiculously majestic creatures on the planet. Well, 270,000 federally protected wild horses have been removed from public lands to make room for cattle grazing. There are more wild horses now in captivity than there are free in the wild. (3) The government kills millions of animals each year because of ranching pressures. (4) Your hard-earned money goes to systematically eliminating these national treasures because they get in the way of feeding other animals garbage food so that they can be slaughtered and turned into more garbage food. It's insane. This should literally be the definition of 'insane' in the Merriam Webster. Who do I write to?

10,000 YEARS AGO, 99% OF BIOMASS (I.E. ZOOMASS) WAS WILD ANIMALS. TODAY, HUMANS AND THE ANIMALS THAT WE RAISE AS FOOD MAKE UP 98% OF THE ZOOMASS.

DAY 8 DRUGS

I know the Internet has taught us to not trust the word "mindblowing" (damn you listicles!) but I'm for real about to blow your mind one more time. Eighty percent of antibiotics sold in the United States go to animals being raised to turn into food. Do you know what that means? Those antibiotics end up in the things you eat and you'll probably grow boobs on your butt one day soon. Or, wait, that will probably be because of the hormones—I'll get to those in a second. First, more on antibiotics because it's so very depressing and this is nothing if not a feel-good book.

Antibiotics, something meant to prevent and treat bacterial infection, something that is hopefully a rarity in most modern people's lives, is continually administered to animals raised for food because of the hellish circumstances they live in. The more we eat animals filled with these antibiotics, the higher our resistance to them becomes, and that's not good. Not to get all alarmist on you, but as of 2014, antibiotic-resistant bacteria infects two million Americans every year, causing at least 23,000 deaths (5), and it's only going to get worse. If we continue down this path, we're headed straight for a worldwide epidemic that will be later immortalized in an end-of-days-holy-shit-humanity-is-effed disaster flick. It'll probably be a really fun movie, but the reality is gonna be terrifying.

And what about hormones? Currently, six different steroidal hormones are approved by the FDA to be administered to animals used for food to bulk them up faster than food alone—the natural hormones estradiol, progesterone, testosterone, and the synthetic hormones trenbolone acetate, progestin melengestrol acetate, and zeranol. (2) These hormones have been associated with early puberty for girls (fun!) and increased risk of certain cancers. (3)

And it doesn't end there, animals are raised on a diet of grains grown with pesticides—to control the intestinal parasites and other gross things that invade bodies when living in cramped, shitty environments—and the residue accumulates in the animals' fatty tissue and milk. Since approximately 80% of the corn and 22% of the wheat produced in the United States every year is used for animal feed, while 30 million tons of US-produced soy meal is consumed annually as livestock feed, and it's all grown in intensive industrial farming operations that often rely heavily on insecticides and herbicides. And then you consume it! Yum!

And, of course, what you don't consume (and the residue of what you do consume) ends up running off into our environment and hugely contributing to the toxic world we live in. Ugh, I can't even joke about how sad this is. I want my grand-children to be able to breathe air and swim in streams and live the life I never did because I'm too lazy! Come on, humanity. Think of my unborn children and how much they deserve all the things because they're gonna be so cute. (Because I'm gonna choose what they look like; that'll be a thing by 2050, right?) (JK, I'll love my grandbabies even if they're uggos.)

DAY 9
VEGANIC

You can take your head out of your hands and stop your convulsing sobs: we've made it to a not so awful chapter. Hooray us! Pat yourself on the back with a carrot because we're about to talk about Environmental Farming, otherwise technically known as "veganic farming". Veganic, or vegan organic, is a type of farming that shuns all artificial chemicals (pesticides and other funky stuff) and animal products (such as bloodmeal, fish products, bone meal, feces (1), which, in itself, is often filled with gross surprises like antibiotics) in favor of creating gorgeous, fertile soil the natural way and growing the most beautiful fruits and veggies you've ever seen.

This method of farming creates and maintains fertile land by using vegetable compost, green manures, crop rotation, mulches, and other sustainable and ecologically superior growing methods.(2) As for the results? Hold on to your hats, because this dish is delish. If you want a lesson in how looks can be deceiving, do a side-by-side taste test of a conventionally grown tomato and one from a veganic farm. The former tastes like it was grown on garbage island and then simmered in PigPen's armpits; the veganically grown tomato tastes like something mother nature herself bore from her delicious bosom and then passed through heaven on its way to your mouth. Your taste buds come to life and then physically slap you in the face for keeping them away from such fresh, juicy, perfectly plump fruit and veggies. Veganic farming should be the future if we want our future to be the most delicious thing in all of space and time.

Now that you're about to sell off your loved ones for a taste of veganic produce, you should know that you don't have to sacrifice dear Aunt Jean just to eat some life-changing leeks. Veganic farming is easy and fun! All you need is some vegan, organic compost, mulch, and/or ash—think fruit/vegetable peels, leaves, grass clippings, hay mulch, and wood ash. These things will nurture healthy soil and grow the most gorgeous greens you've ever seen (or, more importantly, tasted). When you're ready to get started, the Internet offers a plethora of resources to turn your thumb a vibrant shade of green. (Just don't search "veganic porn". I took the bullet on that one so you don't have to.) (Please no questions about why I Googled that in the first place. I have no good answer for you.)

DID YOU KNOW?
BLOOD AND BONES FROM SLAUGHTERHOUSES ARE USED IN GROWING PLANT FOOD! BUT THERE IS ANOTHER WAY! VEGANIC FARMING!

Annnnd back to the depressing stuff! Let's talk a little more about ocean dead zones because they're so horrific, it cannot be overstated. (It's OK; when this book is done, I'm totally gonna buy you a coconut milk ice cream cone and give you a pony.) But first, I need to pollute your entire brain with the awfulness of ocean dead zones! Much like the human species is doing to our oceans. Oceans, which cover over 71% of the Earth's surface, are enormous eco-systems that we know little about. Well, except that they're filled with magical creatures, our garbage, and magical creatures choking on our garbage.

Dead zones, or "hypoxic" (meaning "lacking oxygen") zones, are areas where the chemical nutrients in the water are so heightened that it leads to excessive algae bloom that depletes the water of oxygen and thus kills everything living in the area. The leading cause of ocean dead zones? You're catching on! It's nitrogen and phosphorous from agricultural runoff (AKA antibiotic filled animal crap, ammonia, and other disease causing pathogens from factory farms)! (1) For example, the dead zone off of the Gulf of Mexico. This 8,500 square mile swath (about the size of New Jersey) is not far from where the Mississippi river drains into the gulf, and guess what the Mississippi river is filled with? Runoff from factory farms up and down the Midwest. (2) It's crazy that a factory farm in Missouri suffocates ocean life off of Mexico but hey, life is crazy. Also depressing.

Lucky for us, dead zones are not permanent things. Or, at least, they don't have to be. If we stopped the pollution—i.e. ended our dependence on meat, dairy, and eggs—the ecosystems could rebuild and we could all live on a planet where dolphins can swim and eat wherever they like. And isn't that what we all want? Dolphins everywhere forever? That's rhetorical because duh. (Plus, don't forget about the ice cream and pony I promised you.)

CHECK OUT THE VEGAN SUSHI RECIPE IN THIS BOOK FOR AWESOME OCEAN SAVING FOOD

LIVESTOCK OPERATIONS ON LAND HAVE CREATED MORE THAN 500 NITROGEN FLOODED DEADZONES AROUND THE WORLD IN OUR OCEANS.

GOVERNMENT AND LOBBY INVOLVEMENT

Now you're thinking, "but isn't our government looking out for us?!" and to that I say, here's a smack upside the head and a little civics lesson. No, the government is not doing anything for you because you are small potatoes and nobody cares about the animals because they don't have a lot of money to curry favor on Capitol Hill. (Thanks for nothing, Scrooge McDuck!)

You see, the people in power have a vested interest in keeping the status quo. They make moola handoverfist at the expense of the environment, our health, the animals, and their own employees and nothing is done about it because they have giant pocketbooks and powerful lobbyists.

There are a myriad of ways in which our government is an active participant in the destruction of our environment via animal agriculture, ranging from its hefty subsidies for meat, eggs, and dairy (and the crops that support meat, eggs, and dairy) and incredible amounts of asinine legislation.

WHEN TAKING INTO ACCOUNT HIDDEN EXTERNAL COSTS, A $4 BIG MAC WOULD COST AROUND $12

For example, a Big Mac from McDonald's costs $4.56, but when you factor in the hidden, externalized expenses, i.e. associated healthcare costs, government subsidies, and environmental damage, they should be more like $12 a pop. (4) Would you pay that much for a salt lick of pesticides, mucked up waterways, and animal cruelty? You're not a nutball, so probably not. And it gets worse. When it comes to meat as an industry, the government spends $557 million a year for animal agriculture to promote their food to the public. From 1995 to 2010, of the $200 billion spent to subsidize U.S. commodity crops, roughly 2/3 went to animalfeed crops, tobacco and cotton. To compare, no regular direct subsidies were given to fruits or vegetables. (5)

And then there's the introduction and passage of "AgGag" bills. These bills are attempts to censor whistleblowers, investigators, and journalists who expose atrocities committed against the environment and animals on factory farms and slaughterhouses. They literally make it illegal to publish and distribute footage of these horrific places, further allowing big ag to do whatever they want, consequences be damned. (1)

Even more terrifying, the Animal Enterprise Terrorism Act (AETA), passed in 2006, prohibits anyone from engaging in conduct "for the purpose of damaging or interfering with the operations of an animal enterprise." (2) Basically, it gives the U.S. Department of Justice greater authority to target activists. Who supported this bill? National Association for Biomedical Research, Fur Commission USA, GlaxoSmithKline, Pfizer, Wyeth, United Egg Producers, National Cattlemen's Beef Association and many more. A noble crew, to be sure. (JK, these people are human garbage.) (3)

"But that's so messed up!" you're saying, and you're not wrong. But the fact remains that we do nothing about it and the fat cats on Capitol Hill eat a bunch of steak and laugh all the way to the bank, while the rest of us rot from the animal flesh and animal secretions we are being sucked into consuming. U.S.A! U.S.A! U.S.A!

DAY 12: ORGANIC MYTH

AHH, ORGANIC FOOD—THE MAGIC PILL THAT ABSOLVES RICH PEOPLE FROM WORRYING ABOUT WHERE THEIR FOOD COMES FROM. MANY BELIEVE IF YOU LISTEN TO NPR, DRIVE A PRIUS, AND BUY ORGANIC, YOU'RE BASICALLY SAVING THE WORLD SINGLE HANDEDLY AND DESERVE - PARADES IN YOUR HONOR. UNFORTUNATELY, THE MYTH OF ORGANIC MEAT SOMEHOW BEING HEALTHIER AND MORE ENVIRONMENTALLY FRIENDLY IS JUST THAT: A MYTH.

99% OF THE MEAT AMERICANS EAT IS FROM FACTORY FARMS. SO, RIGHT OFF THE BAT, IF YOU'RE NOT ROLLING IN MONEY AND ACCESSIBILITY, YOU'RE PRETTY MUCH DESTINED TO AN ETERNITY OF ANTIBIOTICS, HORMONES, AND ARSENIC TAINTED MEATS. FURTHER, IT'S AN IDEA THAT CANNOT SCALE. TO RAISE HEALTHY ORGANIC ANIMALS, YOU NEED A LOT OF SPACE AND RESOURCES AND IT'S JUST NOT FEASIBLE, NOR IS IT WORTH IT.

AND THAT'S JUST THE BEGINNING: THERE ARE A MYRIAD OF OTHER PROBLEMS WITH ACTING LIKE EATING ORGANIC DEAD ANIMALS IS AN ACCEPTABLE ALTERNATIVE TO FACTORY FARMS. FOR EXAMPLE, ORGANICALLY RAISED CHICKENS MAY SUFFER FROM MANY MORE DISEASES THAN THOSE PUMPED FULL OF ANTIBIOTICS BECAUSE, SURPRISE, THE ANTIBIOTICS KEEP THE CONVENTIONALLY RAISED CHICKENS FROM DROPPING DEAD.

Animals dropping dead from disease is pretty common on over crowded organic farms. Animals being deprived medicine that they actually need is also a common occurrence because the farmer wants to sell their milk. Oh, and yeah, even though their waste isn't tainted with drugs like the stuff from conventional lots, the runoff of (literal) crap is still a huge strain on our environment.

Beyond that, finding animals who were truly raised on a 100% organic diet is damn near impossible—even cows raised on organic farms are sent to conventional feedlots to fatten up before slaughter. Oh, and by the way, they're all sent to the same factory slaughterhouses, so it's not as if the organic steak you're eating came from a cow who was read a bedtime story before the farmer cuddled her to death. Nope, the animals having the "privilege" of being raised organic die in the same disease infested slaughterhouses as the rest of 'em.

BUT, YOU KNOW, ENJOY THAT STEAK!

DID YOU KNOW: EATING GRASS-FED ANIMALS IS EVEN MORE UNSUSTAINABLE!

DAY 13: EGG INDUSTRY IMPACT

"Fine!" you're thinking. "I won't eat meat anymore! PLEASE JUST LEAVE ME ALONE!" and my response to that is, "Nope. We've only just begun." Mua ha ha! Taps fingers together like a Bond Villain and takes another sip of green juice. We might be here all night. Let's talk eggs. Those delicious chicken abortions you love to fry in grease and slide down your gullet because that's what you've done forever and it's your God given right as an "Amurican".

Well, I'm sorry to tell you this but eggs are garbage and absolutely awful for the environment. Sure, they're not as terrible as eating an entire cow, but they're far from OK. For starters, to get a kilogram of egg protein (what you'd get from about 10 dozen eggs) you need roughly the same amount of land that you'd need to get the same about of protein from pork or chicken. (1) In that space, chickens are stuffed into cramped wire laying cages, unable even to expand their wings, and in that environment is where things like antibiotics come in handy to keep them from dying under such unnatural conditions. And since the food energy input (i.e. dietary energy intake) to output (i.e. total energy expenditure) for eggs is 39:1; (3) meaning it takes approximately 39 calories of energy to produce 1 calorie of egg. That's a pretty ineffective way to get our calories on, my friend. And if this life isn't about consuming delicious calories, I don't want to know. Food is so good. Like, especially french fries. OK, back to business!

Interestingly, these cramped conditions that provide a hellish life for layer hens are the same awful conditions that help to somewhat reduce the environmental footprint of eggs. (2) Because the chickens can't move and are stacked on top of each other (pecking each other's eyes out!), they use less energy. Therefore, in this instance, free range eggs are less environmentally friendly because of their land and resource usage and pollution. So, here's your choice: destroy the environment by eating eggs from so-called free range birds (news flash: free range animals don't lead happy lives!) or eat liquid antibiotic bombs from a chicken who plucked her own feathers out from stress (but has a smaller impact on the environment.) I know, it's like trying to choose between apple pie and an ice cream sundae for dessert! So hard!! (Actually, it's more like trying to pick between garbage pie and a shit sundae, but you know.)

WIERD FACT:
Due to decades of genetic manipulation and selective breeding, hens produce up to 300 eggs per year. In nature, wild hens lay only up to 15 eggs annually, and only during breeding season.

DID YOU KNOW?
EATING ONE EGG PER DAY IS THE EQUIVELENT OF SMOKING 5 CIGARETTES PER DAY IN TERMS OF CAUSING PREMATURE DEATH!

DAY 14: RED MEAT VS WHITE MEAT

You probably know quite a few people (hi mom!) who have cut beef and pork from their diets in an effort to decrease their environmental footprint. That's awesome! But what's not awesome is when those same people eat extra chicken and fish instead (hi mom!), because really, that's not helping the planet as much as my mom thinks it is. That's because the environmental impact of chicken and fish production is still pretty awful, and much worse than just eating a bunch of delicious food that wasn't once marinated in their own filth. Enjoy, mom!

Want to hear some disturbing information to help you realize that all animal consumption is horrific for the environment? Oh, good! I thought you'd never ask. (You didn't, but still I keep going.) Pigs produce 10 times the waste of humans and are a major contributor to aquatic dead zones in North Carolina and the great lakes region. Fish farms need five pounds of wild catch fish to produce one pound of farmed fish. And no, wild caught isn't sustainable either — three- quarters of the world's fisheries are already completely exploited. All this turn you off pigs and fish and you're thinking chicken looks pretty good? Well, sorry. Chickens need to eat four pounds of cholesterol-free, fiber-rich grain to produce just one pound of fat, artery-clogging meat.

Yes, red meat is the worst of the worst, but chicken, pork, and fish are also absolutely atrocious, especially considering that you can live a healthier, better, richer, sexier, smarter, and all around more dreamy life by just cutting those "foods" out to begin with. Seriously, there are no environmental winners when it comes to eating animals.

But wait, there's more bad news! (Sob.) Beef uses 28 times more land, 11 times more water, and creates five times more greenhouse gas emissions than pork or chicken. Looking at those numbers makes it seem like it's time to drown yourself in a bucket of dead chicken, but let me really blow your mind. When compared to plant staples like potatoes, wheat, and rice, the impact of beef per calorie is way more egregious, needing 160 times more land and producing 11 times more greenhouse gases. (1) Switch to a PLANeT-based diet and you will literally cut your climate warming emissions in half.

The fact that switching to a PLANeT-based diet isn't a no brainer makes me want to go door to door and shake some sense into all of humanity. Don't test me; I'll do it! But first, let me just eat this giant veggie burger topped with eggplant bacon and guacamole real quick. And maybe some of these polenta fries. Polenta fries are kinda mandatory, right? Oh, and maybe some of this coconut ice cream shake. What? If I'm gonna be kicking ass and taking names for Mother Earth (and I am), I'm gonna need some legit sustenance!

DON'T WORRY ABOUT THE COLOR OF OUR FLESH; WE ARE ALL THE SAME!

SWITCH TO A PLANET-BASED DIET AND YOU WILL LITERALLY CUT YOUR CLIMATE WARMING EMISSIONS IN HALF.

DAY 15
RAINFOREST & LAND USE

Remember when you were a kid and you knew so much about the rainforest? That's a kid thing, right? Like, everyone I know who is a kid or who once was a kid (that's most people, but I'm not putting Benjamin Button on blast here) knows quite a bit about that magical place where tree canopies block out the sun and dew covers every colorful plant and there are mystical creatures. Plus, the Brazilian rainforest is home to a certain tiny fish that can swim into penises, and since that fact once won me a round of bar trivia, I must celebrate it.

Animal agriculture is responsible for up to 91% of Amazon destruction

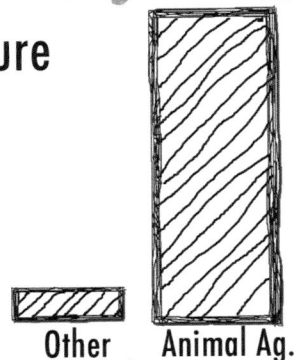

Other   Animal Ag.

Another reason to celebrate it? Oh, it might not be around much longer. You see, animal agriculture is responsible for clearing 136 million rainforest acres. (1) Another fact: up to 91% of Brazilian Amazon destruction has been caused by animal agriculture. (2) Let those enormous numbers sink into your brain. I'll give you a minute. It still hasn't, right? (Let me put it this way: say you baked yourself a cake and I came over and ate 91% of it; how much cake would you have left (and how dead would I be)? The answer is basically none (and very).

Up to 137 plant, animal and insect species are lost every day due to rainforest destruction.

Every second of every day, up to one to two acres of rainforest are cleared. (3) 110 plant, animal, and insect species are lost every day due to rainforest destruction. (4) The leading causes of this destruction? Livestock and feed crops. (5) We are literally destroying one of the most precious natural resources on this earth because we want to eat some crappy hamburger. Maybe I have a tiny baby brain (not gonna argue I don't!), but no matter how many times I see or read those numbers, my mind refuses to process it. Like, in the time it took me to write this much, hundreds of acres of irreplaceable resources have been completely destroyed—wiped from this earth forever. Heartbreaking isn't strong enough of a word; there's nothing that can properly explain the enormity of this injustice.

Oh, and you know the rich people who think they deserve a parade because they only buy grassfed beef? Well, so sad, too bad, grass is even worse for the environment than grain because it takes so much more land to feed a cow. So, really, grassfed beef should be called rainforestfed beef, and I hope the Scrooge McDuck who brags about how good his grassfed burger is can sleep well at night knowing that he probably wiped out an entire species for his snack.

But ha ha grass fed organic burgers and bacon are soooo good. Blah blah blah.

DAY 16 OCEAN DEPLETION & SUSTAINABLE FISH

How many of you know a "vegetarian" who eats fish? Now, how many of you have been a "vegetarian" who eats fish? You're all raising your hands, aren't you? I know you are, because it's an epidemic—the amount of people who think fish is a vegetable has me seriously concerned about our public school system. (No, there's no such thing as a pescatarian; please sit down.)

That said, it's not that hard to see why some people do this. Hell, I did for a while. It's a lot easier to feel empathy for a pig (so cute!) or a cow (those eyes!) than it is for weird ol' fish just swimming and peeing in that great big terrifying ocean of ours. Knowing that, it's not hard to see why threefourths of the world's fisheries are totally exploited. (1)

Overfishing has brought many of our fish populations to the brink of collapse—and beyond. We pull 90 million tons of fish from our oceans each year. (2) And the more grotesque part is that most of it, we're not even eating! For every pound of fish caught, an average of five pounds of species the fishers didn't intend to catch, or bykill, is tossed out. (3)

3/4 OF THE WORLD'S FISHERIES ARE EXPLOITED OR DEPLETED.

To break it down even further, as much as 40% of fish caught globally every year is discarded. (4) That's 63 billion pounds of animals dead for no reason. And that's not all: scientists estimate as many as 650,000 whales, sharks, dolphins and seals are killed every year by fishing vessels. (5) It's interesting that most people are horrified by shark fin soup, but the majority of sharks are killed during normal fishing practices. So, if you're against shark fin soup and dolphin tuna, you should be against all fishing.

I know we can all agree that whales, dolphins, and seals are the triumvirate of magical sea creatures and the knowledge that over half a million of them die every year simply for getting in the way of some shitty tuna casserole is a travesty that's hard to wrap your mind around. By some estimates, we'll have fishless oceans as early as 2054, and many say that once the oceans die, we all die. What's currently happening in our oceans is more terrifying than any horror film Hollywood has even dreamt up, and I'm including "Jaws" here, which made me literally pee my pants in middle school. (No, I didn't have a ton of friends.)

As corny as it is to say this: only we can. Only if we stop supporting the businesses that are doing this will they stop. Fish, even though they are weird and foreign to us, are still an important part of the health of this planet and it's our responsibility to stop ruining everything. Besides, the more you think about it, the more you realize that fish are actually dope sentient beings who can breathe underwater. I mean, come on. That is rad.

90-100 million tons of fish are pulled from our oceans each year.

DAY 17: MEATONOMICS

I THINK WE CAN ALL AGREE BY NOW HOW DEAD ANIMALS AND ANIMAL BYPRODUCTS ARE SYSTEMATICALLY MURDERING THE ENTIRE EARTH. SO, WHY WOULD YOU EAT IT STILL? OH, BIG MACS ARE CHEAP AND VEGETABLES COST ALL THE MONEY! WELL, FIRST OF ALL, BIG MACS AREN'T THAT CHEAP WHEN COMPARED TO A LOT OF OTHER FOODS THAT AREN'T ACTIVELY TRYING TO GIVE YOU A HEART ATTACK.

$414 billion in externalized cost from animal agriculture!

IN HIS BOOK MEATONOMICS, LAWYER AND ADVOCATE FOR SUSTAINABLE CONSUMPTION, DAVID ROBINSON SIMON USES THINGS LIKE FACTS AND LOGIC TO SHOW THE HIDDEN COSTS THE ANIMAL FOOD SYSTEM IMPOSES ON TAXPAYERS, ANIMALS AND THE ENVIRONMENT. TURNS OUT, THESE COSTS TOTAL ABOUT $414 BILLION YEARLY. FOR EVERY $1 WORTH OF MEAT AND DAIRY PRODUCERS SELL, THEY IMPOSED ALMOST $2 IN HIDDEN COSTS ON US THROUGH ARTIFICIALLY LOW PRICES, INFLATED SUBSIDIES, AND HEAVY CONTROL OVER LEGISLATION AND REGULATION.

FOR EXAMPLE, US TAXPAYERS SPEND AN INCREDIBLE 38 BILLION ANNUALLY TO SUBSIDIZE MEAT AND DAIRY, WHICH JUST KEEPS GETTING CHEAPER AND CHEAPER BECAUSE OF IT. (GO AHEAD AND FIND A REFERENCE OF ANOTHER U.S. SPENDING TOTAL TO COMPARE HOW RIDICULOUS THAT AMOUNT IS!) IN 1935, THE US RETAIL PRICE OF A POUND OF CHICKEN WAS $5.07 (ADJUSTED FOR INFLATION) AND IN 2011, IT WAS $1.34. DO THOSE NUMBERS SOUND RIGHT TO YOU? AND EVEN WORSE, OUR RELIANCE ON MEAT —U.S. PER CAPITA CONSUMPTION OF CHICKEN AND OTHER MEAT EXCEEDS WORLD AVERAGE BY 3—IS KILLING US. THE UNITED STATES SPENDS $314 BILLION TO TREAT DISEASES RE-LATED TO MEAT AND DAIRY CONSUMPTION. THESE NUMBERS SHOULD DEEPLY DISTURB ALL OF US BECAUSE THEY'RE DEEPLY DISTURBING. MEAT IS LITERALLY COSTING US OUR LIVES AND WE'RE PAYING THE IN-DUSTRY FOR THE PRIVILEGE. IT'S LIKE WE'RE SIMULTANEOUSLY COATING OUR ARTERIES WITH LARD WHILE TAKING A CRAP ON THE AMAZON THEN HANDING OVER ALL OF OUR MONEY TO SOME ANIMAL FOOD SYSTEM BEFORE SHOOTING OURSELVES IN THE FACE. NOT TO BE DRAMATIC OR ANYTHING.

In 1935, the US retail price of a pound of chicken was $5.07 (adjusted for inflation) in 2011, it was $1.34. Do those numbers sound right to you?

HOLY COW!
70 BILLION FARMED ANIMALS ARE REARED ANNUALLY WORLDWIDE. MORE THAN 6 MILLION ANIMALS ARE KILLED FOR FOOD EVERY HOUR. ...NO WONDER IT'S BIG BUSINESS

DAY 18: FOOD SUPPLY AND STARVATION

SORRY THAT I HAVE TO BREAK YOUR HEART RIGHT NOW, BUT THIS MIGHT BE THE SADDEST OF THE SAD CHAPTERS. IN THIS WORLD, ALMOST ONE BILLION PEOPLE ARE ON THE VERGE OF STARVATION EVERY DAY, AND 21,000 PEOPLE (MOSTLY KIDS) DIE EVERY DAY FROM HUNGER OR HUNGER-RELATED DISEASES. WHILE THIS IS HAPPENING, WE CONTINUE TO FEED CLOSE TO HALF OF THE WORLD'S GRAIN TO LIVESTOCK. THERE ARE 7.2 BILLION PEOPLE ON EARTH, AND WE GROW ENOUGH GRAIN TO FEED 10 BILLION PEOPLE, AND YET, PEOPLE ARE DYING BECAUSE OF LACK OF FOOD. IN SOME PLACES, GRAIN AND MEAT IS EXPORTED TO MEET DEMANDS IN OTHER PARTS OF THE COUNTRY OR WORLD, WHILE THEIR CITIZENS STARVE. IN THE UNITED STATES ALONE, IF WE FED THE GRAIN CURRENTLY GIVEN TO LIVESTOCK DIRECTLY TO PEOPLE, WE COULD FEED NEARLY 800 MILLION PEOPLE. (3)

IT'S A COMPLEX ISSUE WITH MANY FACTORS AT PLAY—CORRUPT GOVERNMENTS, EVIL CORPORATIONS, AND EXTREME POVERTY ALL PLAY THEIR PART, BUT ANIMAL AGRICULTURE PLAYS A MAJOR ROLE BECAUSE IT USES RESOURCES THAT COULD BE FED DIRECTLY TO HUMANS. AND INCREASING MEAT PRODUCTION ISNT THE ANSWER BECAUSE THE CROPS GROWN TO FEED ANIMALS COULD GO DIRECTLY TO PROVIDING SUSTAINABLE NOURISHMENT FOR LOCAL PEOPLE. WE'RE LITERALLY TAKING FOOD FROM COMMUNITIES THAT NEED IT, AND SENDING IT ELSEWHERE TO FATTEN UP COWS FOR SLAUGHTER SO THEY CAN BE KILLED AND SERVED IN A NUTRIENT VOID FAST FOOD BURGER TO SOMEONE HALFWAY ACROSS THE COUNTRY/WORLD. DO ANY OF YOU WORK AT WEBSTER'S DICTIONARY? BECAUSE THAT SHOULD BE THE LITERAL DEFINITION OF INSANITY, AND WE NEED TO FIX IT.

1.5 ACRES CAN PRODUCE 37,000 POUNDS OF PLANT—BASED FOOD.
1.5 ACRES CAN ONLY PRODUCE 375 POUNDS OF MEAT.

82% OF STARVING CHILDREN LIVE IN COUNTRIES WHERE FOOD IS FED TO ANIMALS. AND THE ANIMALS ARE EATEN BY WESTERN COUNTRIES.

ONE ACRE OF LAND CAN YEILD

- 50,000 pounds of tomatoes
- 53,000 pounds of potatoes
- 30,000 pounds of carrots
- OR ONLY 250 pounds of beef

TO TURN THINGS AROUND IS A MULTI-PRONGED PROCESS, BUT ONE THING WE DEFINITELY NEED TO DO IS GET FOOD DIRECTLY TO THE PEOPLE. THAT WOULD ERADICATE HUNGER AND THEN SOME! THAT WOULD MEAN WELL-NOURISHED KIDS GOING TO SCHOOL FEELING HEALTHY AND STRONG, ACING TESTS, BECOMING ASTRONAUTS, AND BUILDING NEW CIVILIZATIONS FOR US IN OUTER SPACE BECAUSE WE WANT TO LIVE IN OUTER SPACE, NOT BECAUSE WE'RE FORCED TO LIVE THERE BECAUSE OUR PLANET IS BURIED UNDER A MOUNTAIN OF GARBAGE.

Growing feed crops for livestock consumes 56% of water in the US.
Source: Center for Science in the Public Interest

DAY 19:
SOCIAL IMPACTS

There are innumerable ways in which eating a PLANeT-based diet (You're welcome to steal that expression and/or pretend I never wrote it! Your choice!) helps not only the Earth, but also the people on it. Now let's get into it because you're a busy, important, attractive person who probably has somewhere to be.

First, cutting out animal products frees up grain normally fed to livestock and allows it to go directly to people; feeding them healthier food at a fraction of the cost. The truth is, 1.5 acres can produce either 37,000 pounds of plant-based food or 375 pounds of meat. (1) What's the better choice here? If you think it's meat, you might be the Hamburglar. Please note: If you are the Hamburglar, I'm sorry, but you need to know: you're the worst and maybe you should start stealing something less disgusting than McDonald's hamburgers? Like hot nuclear garbage, or whatever. Just have a little self respect, you know?

So yeah, as we've established, everyone except for paid fast food spokespeople (and is the Hamburglar a person? It's debatable.) agrees that ending animal consumption will dramatically help the environment, in many ways, and for many people. For example, when you shut down factory farms, that means the end of polluting our air, water, and earth with all those gross chemicals and fecal matter. And that results in healthier environments for all the good folks who live close to those once awful places. Plus, closing them would allow for so many great things, like organic broccoli farms, wilderness preserves, and a myriad of awesome things; maybe we could even return some of the ancestral land to the indigenous communities it was stolen from? If we did things like that, imagine how we'll be mentioned in history books. Instead of "Shitty millennials and their shitty families just shit all over the Earth until it was all gone," it can be all, "Yeah millennials proved they were badass and pretty much saved the day! You're welcome, MOM AND DAD."

Not to mention the end of animal product consumption will lead to a sharp decrease in healthcare costs associated with things like diabetes, high cholesterol, certain cancers, and even more heinous and foul things that I can't bring myself to list because it's so gross and sad. Seriously, freeing yourself from reliance on evil animal products is not only one of the best things you can do for the Earth, it's also one of the best things you can do for yourself. And you're part of the Earth and so I can talk about it in this book because I love you and want you to live forever. I want you to live so long that medical journals study your body to help advance science. That's how much I love you.

1,100 Land activists have been killed in Brazil in the past 20 years.

Day 20:
Backyard Animal Farming Myth to Backyard Gardening

NOW, AT THIS POINT, YOU MIGHT BE FREAKING OUT ABOUT HOW BIG ANIMAL AGRICULTURE IS DESTROYING THE EARTH AND HOLY CRAP, WHAT SHOULD YOU DO?! START YOUR OWN ANIMAL FARM AND GO STRAIGHT OLD MCDONALD ON THE PROBLEM? TO YOU I SAY: PUT DOWN YOUR WHEELBARROW AND STRAW HAT AND LET'S HAVE A TALK. I HAVE SOME BAD NEWS FOR YOU. (BUT FIRST, YOU REALLY THINK YOU COULD KILL A PIG? LIKE, WITH YOUR OWN HANDS? A SWEET, SMART, COOL, WEIRDO PIG WITH HER OWN AWESOME PERSONALITY WHO IS PROBABLY BETTER AT CHECKERS THAN YOU ARE? YOU COULD REALLY KILL THAT PIG?! THAT PIG HAS MORE TO OFFER TO SOCIETY THAN MOST PEOPLE! BUT IF YOU STILL THINK YOU COULD KILL A PIG THAT YOU RAISED FROM A TINY BUNDLE OF PIGLET CUTENESS TO SMART, CUDDLY, PROUD PIG ADULT, THEN YOU DO YOU.

NO MATTER WHAT URBAN FARMING "EXPERTS" NOVELLA CARPENTER OR MICHAEL POLLAN SAY, BACKYARD CHICKENS AREN'T GONNA SAVE THE WORLD. SURE, MAYBE THEY CAN PROVIDE A FEW EGGS TO RICH, BORED PEOPLE LIVING IN WHATEVER HIPSTER NEIGHBORHOOD THEY'RE CURRENTLY GENTRIFYING (THAT IS, UNTIL THE CHICKENS GET ATTACKED BY LOCAL RACCOONS AND DIE SLOW, PAINFUL DEATHS!), BUT THEY'RE NOT A SUSTAINABLE SOLUTION FOR 99.9999% OF THE POPULATION WHO DOESN'T HAVE A PHD FROM BERKELEY IN BEING SMUG AND RAISING BACKYARD CHICKENS BECAUSE WE'RE BETTER THAN THE REST OF YOU PLEBES.

THERE ARE MANY REASONS BACKYARD ANIMAL FARMING IS A TERRIBLE, ECOLOGICALLY-UNCOOL PROPOSITION, BUT LET ME JUST TACKLE THE MOST PRESCIENT ONES BECAUSE MY FINGERS WILL FALL OFF FROM RAGE TYPING IF I HAVE TO DO THIS ALL DAY. FIRST, THE FEED THAT YOU GIVE ANIMALS RAISED IN YOUR BACKYARD ANIMAL FARM ISN'T ALSO GROWN IN YOUR BACKYARD, SO YOU'RE ALREADY CONTRIBUTING TO THE ECOLOGICAL FOOTPRINT YOU CLAIM TO SO ABHOR. SECONDLY, GROWING FRUIT AND VEGGIES IN YOUR BACKYARD IS SMART BECAUSE 1.5 ACRES CAN PRODUCE 37,000 POUNDS OF PLANT-BASED FOOD, WHILE THE SAME FOOTPRINT CAN PRODUCE ONLY 375 POUNDS OF MEAT. (1) SO YEAH, YOUR RAISED BOXES OF CHARD AND KALE ARE SO WORTH IT. PLUS, VEGANS CAN FEED THEMSELVES FOR A YEAR ON ONE ACRE OF LAND, WHEREAS A VEGETARIAN TAKES THREE TIMES AS MUCH, AND A MEAT EATER TAKES A WHOPPING 18 TIMES AS MUCH. SO, BASICALLY, I DON'T NEED MUCH SPACE TO LIVE LIKE A FREAKING QUEEN AND THE MEAT-MUNCHING GOOFBALLS NEED A BILLION ACRES (OR WHATEVER) JUST TO RAISE ADORABLE ANIMALS WHOM THEY HAVE TO KILL SO THEY CAN HAVE SOME SUBPAR STEW? HARD PASS. (PLUS, I STILL MAKE STEW, BUT MINE IS ANYTHING BUT SUBPAR. IT'S ABOVE PAR, WHICH I THINK IS A WORD? OR, CLOSE ENOUGH TO A WORD. LET'S JUST EAT.)

1.5 acres can produce 37,000 pounds of plant-based food, while the same footprint can produce only 375 pounds of meat.

DAY 21: GRASS FED MYTH AND WILDLIFE IMPACT

The miracle solution to grainfed feedlot animals that's oft-touted by the foodie elite is the gloriousness of cattle grazing on grass in expansive vistas. Grass feeding, they say, is the more natural, humane, and healthy alternative to animals being forced into feedlots and stuffed full with corn and grain. The way they tell it, you imagine these cows are basically living in Malibu, sipping on kombucha and getting shiatsu massages from Jude Law. But the reality is, we simply don't have the room to do that and Jude Law gives a terrible shiatsu. Look at him; he's too pretty to be good with his hands.

Back to business: Livestock covers 45% of the Earth's total ice-free land. (1) In the United States, nearly half of the contiguous land mass is devoted to animal agriculture. (2) So, yes, all that room that should just be infinity pools and cocktail bars for us is actually tightly packed with animals that are raised to die. (and don't forget their chemicalfilled excrement!) Bummer. Factory farms and their cramped feedlots are many things: depressing, disgusting, disease-ridden death farms, but they're slightly less awful for the environment than grassfed operations. Animals that are grassfed have to live longer, eat extra, and take up significantly more room to acheive sellable standards.

Raising cattle already produces more greenhouse gases than driving cars (3), so what's the sense of increasing that footprint even more, especially when it's not physically possible and the economics of it are impossible. As it stands, we are murdering the Earth at breakneck speed— with 1/3 of the planet already desertified; livestock being the leading driver, naturally (4)—that we just can't afford to further expand the operation.

AMOUNT OF LAND NEEDED IF UNITED STATES SWITCHED TO GRASS FED BEEF

And you gotta ask: when 50% of the contiguous land mass of the United States is being taken up by animal agriculture, what happens to the animals who were there to begin with? Well, it's not an all expenses paid tropical vacation. More like, being systematically slaughtered so they don't interfere with the production of our precious pink slime. Since 2006, more than 26 million wildlife animals - many - endangered! - have been slaughtered by the USDA, because they were competing with land reserved for livestock and other free range farm animals. (5) And no, they don't cuddle them to death, they crush them in traps, poison them with cyanide, gun them down aerially, and trap them in gruesome snares (6). Awesome wildlife aside, many of these grazing areas used to be amazing carbon-sequestering forests. Meaning that when they're cut, burned, and bulldozed to make room for grass-fed grazing, it takes away all that luscious vegetation that helped the Earth thrive.

It's a real horror show, all so we can serve burger bites made with Grade D dead cow to our kids in their crappy school lunches. *Cries self to sleep and floats off on a river of tears to my dreamland where talking dogs play poker with cats in business suits.

DAY 22 – THE REAL LOCAL, SLOW, AND ORGANIC FOOD MOVEMENT

There's something to be said for immersing your hands in soil, tunneling through dirt and planting seeds. I don't know what it is about planting and growing food; I should hate it.

I mean, I don't love being outside because my red hair and ghostly skin will most likely burn to a crisp in about two minutes flat. And the closest I've ever gotten to camping is shopping at an outdoor mall!

But I promise growing fruits and vegetables in your backyard can be easily accomplished and I encourage you to do so! Save the sentient beings and opt to fill your soul by nurturing the light of courageous carrots and kale, juicy fruits, and determined gourds and greens!

Growing food for fun and sustenance is kinda the best. As a reformed black thumb who was basically the Cruella de Vil of houseplants, you need to know that if I can do it, literally anyone can. Like, even babies. I am that pathetic. But I learned that carrots just need some (veganic!) soil, cucumbers just need a little water and sunshine, and kale is basically the heartiest effer on Earth.

JOHN JEAVONS

HOWARD LYMAN

Like, you can come at kale with lack of agua and sporadic sun shine and it's like, "yawn. I'm about to grow so gloriously tall and gorgeously vibrant; you don't even know! p.s. I'm KALE!!! Go away and come back in a week when I'll be good to go in a stirfry K THX, BAI." And that's not even touching on issues of sustainability!

The feed conversion ratio of four pounds of grain to one pound of meat (or higher, considering all the water used and waste produced) is absolutely terrible. Unless you live on a straight up farm, you probably don't have enough room to grow enough food to feed one chicken to produce one egg. Is it worth it? When you could instead have all sorts of other insanely delicious food that's environmentally friendly?

Seriously, growing fruit and vegetables in your backyard is so easy, and you should definitely do it. It's so much more rewarding and less awful than killing a sentient being who you raised since babydom and who trusts you fully, just because you have a hankering for chicken flesh. That's not something you want to do, because that shit is hard, time consuming, and, tbh, pretty disgusting. Oh, and because you have a heart and a brain and probably zoning restrictions on your apartment, you know you can't raise and then slaughter a cow in your backyard, but literally anyone can grow their own food. It's the truest form of slow food, since it can't run away! (I'll take Terrible Dad Jokes for $10,000, Alex.) You can eat organic, amazing food that you grow yourself, and you can eat so much of it. You'll have so many tomatoes that you'll can your own salsa, tomato sauce, and pizza spread and still have plenty to give as holiday gifts. You're basically Betty Crocker, but a real person and not trying to kill other humans with your food.

DAY 23: LIVING BEYOND SELF

Listen, I don't care what anyone says: I love garbage reality TV. Whether it's about hot people pretending to have problems (The Bachelor), talking babies trying to run a corporation (The Apprentice), or someone turning a large ass and a sex tape into a world wide empire (I won't say their names!), I love every second of it. I like the bizarre lives we lead in 2016 in (most of) the United States: I dig running water, flushing toilets, and all sorts of other modern conveniences that separate us from cave people, but there are some sorta dumpy downsides to living like this.

For example, with all the luxuries of this life style, we're so separated from where any thing comes from. The other day I asked my 7 year old niece where vegetables grow and she said, "the supermarket". I have a sinking feeling that if I asked a sampling of my peer group, I'd get the same answer.

THIS CARROT IS AWESOME

We're cut off from the realities of how our world works. Running water is dandy, but do you have any clue where yours comes from or how it gets to you? Flushing toilets are the shit (or the opposite of the shit?) but where does all that waste go? Asking these questions is critical in becoming a good citizen of the Earth, and perhaps the most important one of all is where does our food come from—because it affects every aspect of our lives. Our current animal agriculture system is polluting our food, water, air, and soil beyond recognition—and we're the only ones who can change things. After we open our eyes to the messed up reality of the situation, we can make the empowering choice to take action. We have an exciting ethical opportunity to reject animal agriculture and everything it stands for. We can side with the Earth, and decide to be its ally and its warrior. It allows us to become the true badasses we were meant to be and steward the world into a healthier, happier, sustainable future. And that's what we all want, isn't it? A place for our great great grandkids to post selfies in front of Disneyland (ON MARS). If for nothing else, do it so the future knows the glory that is duck-face.

"YOU CAN CHANGE THE WORLD. YOU MUST CHANGE THE WORLD."
-HOWARD LYMAN

DAY 24: WALKING THE TALK, TALKING THE WALK

NOW THAT YOU'RE FULLY IN THE KNOW ABOUT HOW ANIMAL AGRICULTURE IS MURDERING THE EARTH WITH ITS GREEDY, SLEAZY GROSSNESS, YOU PROBABLY WANT TO GO OUT AND TELL EVERYONE TO STUFF THEIR POT ROAST WHERE THE SUN DON'T SHINE BECAUSE IT'S DOWNRIGHT DESTROYING OUR PLANET. AND SPREADING THIS INFORMATION IS IMPORTANT BECAUSE SAVING THE EARTH IS PROBABLY THE MOST IMPORTANT THING WE CAN DO (OUTSIDE OF HAVING DRINKS AT OUR BECK AND CALL AND PILLOWS MADE OF VEGAN MARSHMALLOWS).BUT, BEFORE YOU TELL YOUR GRANDPA TO GO TO HELL FOR ORDERING AN OMELETTE, LET'S TAKE A DEEP BREATH AND THINK ABOUT HOW TO BEST HELP THE PLANET.

LET ME TELL YOU A LITTLE STORY; THE STORY OF A BABY ACTIVIST NAMED LAURA (NO RELATION) (OK FINE, IT'S ME) AND HER FIRST THANKSGIVING AS A VEGETARIAN. LITTLE LAURA HAD JUST FOUND OUT ALL THE HORRIFIC THINGS THAT HAPPEN TO TURKEYS BEFORE THEY REACH THE KITCHEN TABLE AND IT BASICALLY RIPPED HER HEART OUT AND STOMPED ON IT AND THEN CALLED IT UGLY AND RAN IT OVER WITH A BIG RIG. LITTLE LAURA BELIEVED THAT THE SECOND SHE TOLD HER FAMILY ABOUT ALL THE EFFED UP STUFF THAT HAPPENS TO THE EARTH IN THE NAME OF CORPORATE GREED AND OUR OWN DEEP FRIED TASTE BUDS, THEY'D LOOK AT HER WITH TEARS IN THEIR EYES AND THROW THAT TURKEY OUT THE WINDOW. BUT ALAS, HER SERMON AT THE DINNER TABLE NOT ONLY FELL ON DEAF EARS, IT ALSO TOTALLY ALIENATED EVERYONE WITHIN A FIVE COUNTY RANGE. IT TOOK LIL' LAURA SEVERAL MORE INSANE ENCOUNTERS TO LEARN THAT THE WAY TO HELP PEOPLE UNDERSTAND THE PLIGHT OF THE PLANET IS THROUGH SPREADING THE WORD IN NON-INSANE WAYS; PEOPLE DON'T WANT TO BE GUILTED OR BE MADE TO FEEL LIKE SHIT BECAUSE THEY'RE JUST DOING WHAT EVERYONE ELSE IS DOING.

ask me how you can be this awesome

THE GOOD NEWS ABOUT THIS IS THAT THERE ARE A MILLION OTHER WAYS TO SPREAD THE WORD, AND IT'S ESSENTIAL FOR THE SURVIVAL OF HUMANITY (DRAMATIC! BUT TRUE!) THAT WE SUCCEED. SO YOU NEED TO DO JUST THAT—WHAT ARE YOU GOOD AT? ARE YOU A GOOD BAKER? USE THAT SKILL TO ENLIGHTEN PEOPLE AND SHOW THEM THE LIGHT/A VEGAN CUPCAKE BUFFET. MAYBE YOU'VE NEVER MET A WEBSITE YOU COULDN'T CODE THE CRAP OUT OF? VOLUNTEER YOUR TIME AT NONPROFITS AND HELP BUILD SOMETHING GREAT THAT GETS THE INFORMATION TO MILLIONS. EVERYONE HAS SKILLS, AND EVEN IF YOU'RE LIKE THE MOST USELESS PERSON ON EARTH (BY THE WAY, YOU'RE NOT), YOU CAN STILL SPREAD THE WORD COMPASSIONATELY AMONGST YOUR FRIENDS. JUST DON'T ATTACK OR CALL THEM NAMES (EVEN IF THEY DESERVE IT! SOME PEOPLE DO!), REMEMBER YOU WEREN'T BORN WITH ALL THE SKILLS TO BECOME THE BADASS YOU ARE TODAY.

HELP OTHER PEOPLE BECOME BADASSES WHO GIVE A SHIT ABOUT THEIR WORLD. THEY'LL BE THANKFUL, AND HEY, THEY'LL PROBABLY TELL OTHER PEOPLE. AND THAT'S WHAT WE WANT. AND IF ALL ELSE FAILS, GRAB THEM BY THE SHOULDERS AND SHAKE SOME DAMN SENSE INTO THEM. (JK.) (OK, NOT REALLY; BUT THAT'S LAST RESORT.)

COMPASSION.

PEACE.

JOY.

ANIMAL AGRICULTURE THE #1 POLLUTER!

IT'S A COWSPIRACY!

DAY 25: HOW TO BECOME A VOICE/ACTIVIST

Things I find terrifying: Los Angeles smog (you should not be able to taste the air), The Candyman, red pandas (The stuff of nightmares! They look like ten year old kids in furry costumes!), and leafletting. One of my first activist experiences was leafletting about Earth Day around Union Square in San Francisco and it was the absolute WORST (all caps). Cold talking to people is the most intimidating thing on Earth to me, and I spent the day basically mumbling gibberish and throwing flyers at business people who were judging me. (THEY WERE!) I thought, if this is activism, just shoot me now and bury my body in a pile of shame because no way on this (kinda) green Earth am I doing this garbage again. Interestingly, I went out with my bff that day and he LOVED it; he was engaging with people, starting meaningful conversations, and even got this fancy business lady's phone number. (They dated for several months but then she left him for a Brazilian surfer. She made the right call.)

The point is, when it comes to activism, it's all about finding your passion. I'm decent at flapping my gums (on a computer) and I type fast (70 wpm! bow down!) so writing is what I came around to. But maybe you're better at making and donating money to worthy nonprofits (teach me your ways! I'm so poor!), or you kick ass at organizing parties and so you volunteer to throw an awesome fundraiser. There are a million and one ways to help, and so it's up to you to get creative.

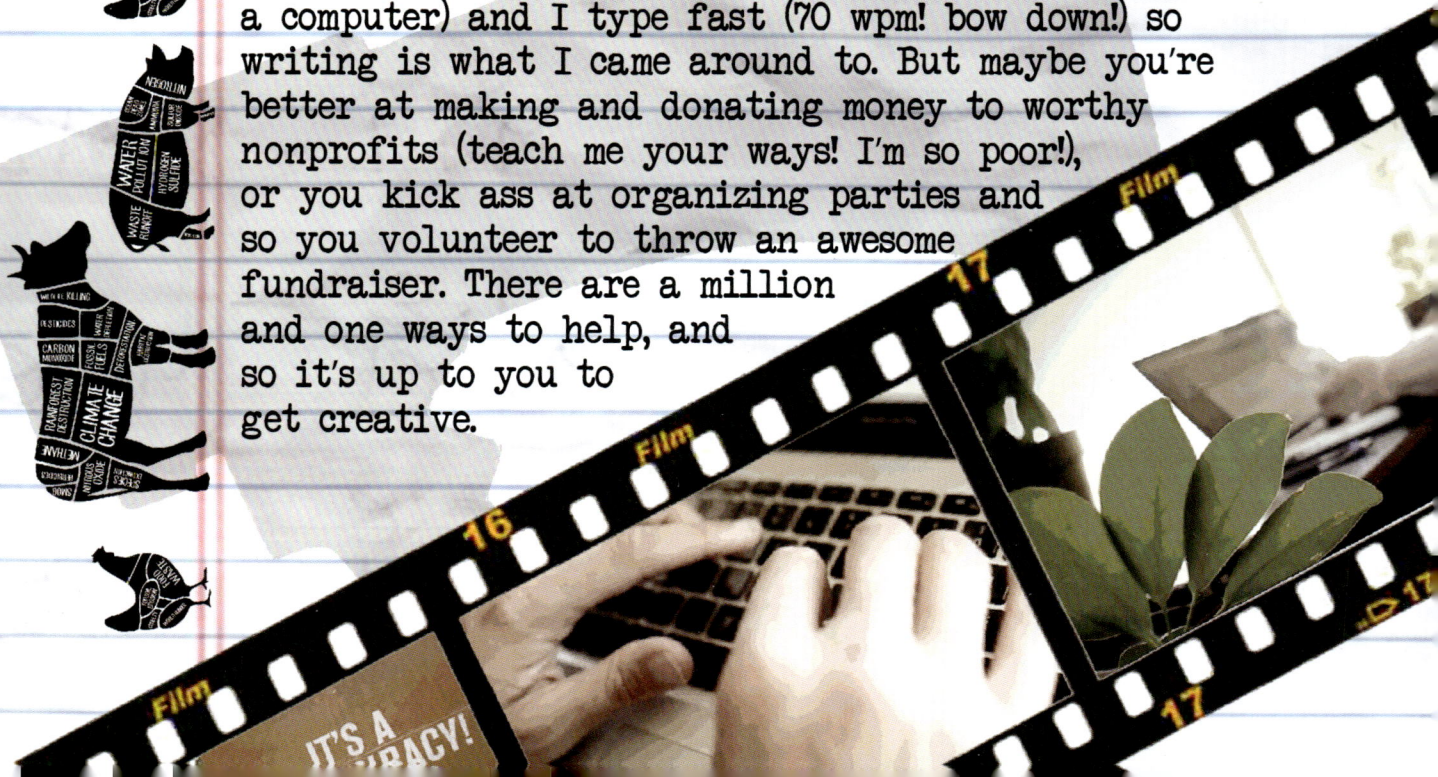

Oh, and I'm sorry if you're stuck in 2006 (no judgment! it was a good year!), but you need social media. Embrace Twitter, Instagram, Facebook, SnapChat, FaceGram, and Instabooty, or what have you. Post delicious vegan recipes, links to positive activism, encourage friends to embrace what makes them special and then use those skills to help save the planet. Use your self(ies) for good! Go crazy, and don't get too fighty because as fun as it is to lay the smack down on some fool in your Facebook feed, you know it'll just make you look like a jerk while simultaneously shortening your life. Scream into a pillow and then hug your cat (JK never hug a cat) and then get back out there and don't give up.

If I'd given up on activism after that one day leafletting (and you know I wanted to; I am not good at rejection because I'm great and everyone needs to understand that), I'd have never found an entire community of buddies online and made a parttime career out of advocating for the environment online and in magazines and newspapers. I wouldn't have the writing career that I have today if it wasn't for giving a shit about something other than myself; and that was just an added bonus! Let's face it, I would probably be eating a Twinkie in a ditch somewhere in Mexico if I hadn't stumbled into this whole wide world of Caring About the Earth (awww). It might sound trite but I didn't truly understand myself and my personal power until I started giving a hoot about something other than myself.

So get out there, find your voice, and sing it out loud and proud. Because you're doing something awesome, and you do deserve a damn parade. With biodegradable balloons. Shaped like pandas. And don't forget my invite or I'll kill you. (Hahaha that's a funny joke!) (Or is it!?) (It is; I'm not actually insane.)

Day 26 – Global Transformation and Shifts

IT'S FUNNY HOW WHEN YOU FIRST ADOPT A PLANET-BASED DIET, PEOPLE CAN BE REAL DING DONGS TOWARDS YOU. ONE OF THE SILLY THINGS YOU'LL HEAR A LOT IS THAT EATING THAT WAY IS ONLY FOR RICH WHITE SNOBS WHO CAN AFFORD TO SPEND THEIR ENTIRE ENORMOUS PAYCHECK BUYING $68 ORGANIC HEIRLOOM BABY CORN GROWN OUT OF NIGELLA LAWSON'S BELLYBUTTON. WELL, YES. THOSE PEOPLE DO EXIST IN THE PLANET-BASED DIET WORLD, BUT THEY ALSO EXIST IN THE MEAT-MOUTH DIET WORLD. YOU CAN'T AVOID JACKHOLES. IT'S JUST PART OF THIS CRAZY LIFE WE'RE ALL LIVING. ON THE WHOLE, THOUGH, EATING PLANTS AND GRAINS COSTS A WHOLE LOT LESS THAN EATING CARCASS (SORRY IF I SPOILED YOUR LUNCH... UNLESS YOUR LUNCH WAS CARCASS). STAPLES LIKE BEANS, RICE, VEGETABLES, AND FRUIT ARE LESS SPENDY THAN STEAK—AND A WHOLE LOT BETTER FOR YOU, TOO. EATING THIS KIND OF DIET IS ALSO EASIER FOR MORE THAN JUST PRIVILEGED WESTERNERS WHO LIVE WITHIN UNICYCLING DISTANCE OF A BIODYNAMIC GROCER, IT'S ALSO POSSIBLE FOR PEOPLE ALL OVER THE WORLD TO GET ACCESS TO THESE CHEAP FOODS ON A REGULAR BASIS.

IF BILLIONS OF PEOPLE IN INDIA AND CHINA HAVE BEEN EATING LIKE THIS FOR CENTURIES, WHY NOT US? BOTH OF THOSE MASSIVE COUNTRIES HAVE SURVIVED AND THRIVED ON A MOSTLY PLANET-BASED DIET FOR A VERY LONG TIME, AND THEY'RE THE BIGGEST SOCIETIES IN HISTORY. IT ISN'T UNTIL FAIRLY RECENTLY THAT MEAT HAS GAINED POPULARITY IN THOSE COUNTRIES—AND BROUGHT THE PROBLEMS ASSOCIATED WITH ITS CONSUMPTION ALONG WITH IT. (1) ADDING MORE MEAT EATERS TO THESE ENORMOUS POPULATIONS WILL HASTEN THE DEMISE OF OUR MOST PRECIOUS RESOURCES. BUH BYE, CLEAN WATER, BREATHABLE AIR, LIVABLE CLIMATES, AND FROLICKING FOREST CREATURES. HELLO, BARREN HELLSCAPE THAT CHOKES US TO DEATH WITH WIND MADE OF GARBAGE AND SEAS MADE OF OIL SLICKS. BE RIGHT BACK, OFF TO STARE INTO THE MEANINGLESS VOID THAT IS OUR CURRENT FUTURE AND CONTEMPLATE THE EMPTINESS OF EXISTENCE. JUST KIDDING, I NEED A SNACK.

LUCKILY, WE CAN CHANGE AND REVERSE THIS GLOBAL DOWNWARD TREND BY HAVING EVERYONE REFOCUS ON A PLANET-BASED DIET. AND YOU CAN BE ONE OF THE FIRST PEOPLE TO MAKE IT HAPPEN, BECAUSE YOU'RE AN AMAZING PIONEER AND A VISIONARY AND ALSO PROBABLY SMELL REALLY GOOD AND PEOPLE JUST WANT TO LISTEN TO YOU, NATURALLY. I KNOW THINGS.

WHAT?

THE FUTURE VISION

DAY. 27

Imagine, if you will, a world with thriving forests, clean rivers, fertile soil, and friendly woodland creatures frolicking about and blowing you kisses. It's a place not unlike something J.R.R. Tolkien envisioned, except without Orlando Bloom and his dreamy flowing locks (so, you know, less wonderful). Sounds lovely, right? Well, that can be where we live. Instead of this stinky factory farm of a polluted planet, we can reverse the damage we've done and create a new world for future humans so that they can fly their cars without fear of crashing into anyone because the air is completely made of dirt and garbage. Kids will be able to maneuver their hoverboards in peace, unafraid that a McRib wrapper will fly directly into their mouth and choke them to death. Wouldn't that be grand? What a time to be alive!

I don't know about you, but if I do have kids (you're welcome, society!), I'd like them to live on a planet that's survivin' and thrivin'. I want my great great grandkids to know what a wild horse looks like because they saw one roaming free, and what a koala looks like because they peered up at a eucalyptus tree at the exact right moment, and not because there's now a display at the Natural History Museum on "Australian Animals That Are Extinct Because Humans Are Actual Trash". I want them to be able to swim in their oceans and explore their woods and I want the air to be clean enough to breathe and for their food not to give them diseases. Is this too much to ask? That we leave the world a little better than we found it? Because, at this point, we're really not, and I don't want to be remembered as the generation that irreversibly screwed over the Earth and all its inhabitants. I want to be part of the generation that brought the world the most terrible music and wore the ugliest clothes but also gave the most craps about the planet. That wouldn't be the worst way to be remembered. (Just please know that I personally had nothing to do with Nickelback. I want that added to the Constitution.)

FUTUREVISION

Phew. We've covered a lot of ground so far and I'm a little sleepy because being right all the time makes you tired. Well, maybe it's called being a blowhard—potaytoe, po-tahtoe. Anyway: glad you're here! Pat yourself on the back for getting this far, but your journey isn't over yet! Now we must talk about the ways in which we're all going to take what we learned and use that information to create positive change in the world. This is when we need to pull on our big girl pants and get down to business.

Our responsibility to the Earth goes beyond just adopting a delicious PLANeT-based diet, which is important, but, honestly, not enough. I know, I'm like the coach who tells you there's only one more lap to run and then is all "PSYCH! Give me ten more because I'm the WORST!" But don't think of this as a burden, think of it as an exciting ethical opportunity to be a superhero for the planet. You're like Superwoman without the sexist (and frankly, hideous) spandex. By figuring out how to use your talents and skills to help more people understand that creating a healthier planet is in all our best interests, you ensure your gold medal in the Give a Crap Olympics. And because that has real ramifications for our world and the people on it, it's worth more than other Olympic medals. (Except on eBay or other places where things of monetary value are sold.)

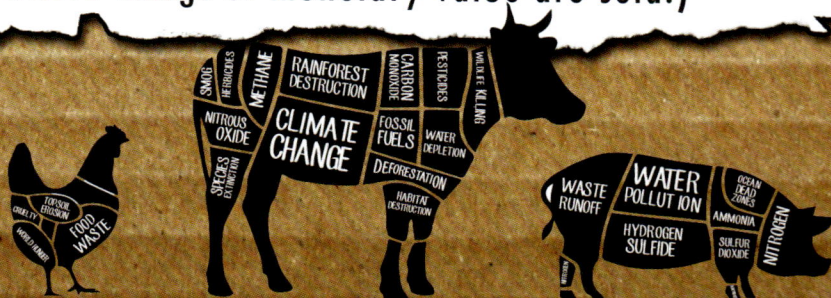

Unfortunately for both of us, I can't tell you the exact way in which you're best suited to helping the cause. If I knew you, I'd totally tell you what to do because I am super bossy, but since I don't, I need you to get bossy on yourself. Take a moment and sit with yourself—ask "how can I best spread the word and help the Earth?" Whether it's organizing, volunteering, recruiting, coding, cooking, or a million other things you can come up with on your own because you are not only very good-looking but also hyper-intelligent, you have the absolute power to effect real change using everything you already are. You're an amazing asset that the Earth is blessed to have, so get out there and let the world know it. Mother Nature and all her creatures will thank you—maybe even in the form of puppy kisses. Damn, you're lucky.

DAY 29

relax and enjoy life (and food)

As we've talked about before, when I first adopted a PLANeT-based diet, I was the absolute worst. But after nearly ruining some important friendships and almost giving myself a rage stroke, I decided to calm the eff down before I had a heart attack in the middle of the 101 because I didn't like someone's twee bumper sticker. But life's way too precious to waste being a total psycho grump. Plus, let's be real, it's kinda nuts and truly magical that we're alive—we're literally awesome freaks of nature that won a million little lotteries to even be born. And here we are, just strutting around on this flying space rock like the badasses that we are. We should be happy that we won this big prize and get to experience all the wonderful things that make up a life.

If you're happy in your life, then you'll be an even more amazing advocate for the Earth. I know, I know, but hear me out: I love that professional sadsack Charlie Brown, but I don't want to share a sixpack and some veggie dogs with him, you know? People want to be around happy, positive people, and if they want to be around you, they'll listen to what you're saying. Being content in your own life will make you a much better advocate for the planet, and it'll probably get you laid. JK, not everything is about sex. Just most things.

The point is: life is great and you're great and let's throw ourselves a party to celebrate. One with some amazing PLANeT-based tacos because tacos are basically manna from heaven and should be revered as such and eaten at all times. And, you know, if you buy some non PLANeT-based cheese accidentally to eat with them, don't beat yourself up about it. Transitioning to this diet is going to come with some screw-ups because we're human and that's what we do. Next time just buy (or make!) some of the PLANeT-based stuff and you're golden. Like most things worth fighting for, it's a process of wins and setbacks, but the important thing is to give yourself a hug (aww) and keep moving forward. Remember that you're here for the planet, and it doesn't matter if you make some mistakes—what matters is that you stay the (righteous, awesome, badass) course. (Also, I'm sorry. Biting into a salt lick when you think you're about to eat a tasty brownie is the worst thing that has ever happened to anyone, no exaggeration. So maybe someone should stop you? Live all your dreams...except that one.)

SETTLE IN & ROCK ON!

Here's the thing: You're awesome. Well, that's the first thing. Here's a second thing: Every time you make the decision to eat a PLANeT-based meal, you're not only making a very delicious decision (because PLANeT-based food is very delicious), but one that's ensuring the existence of humans on this planet for millenniums to come. What's more delicious than that? Besides peanut butter chocolate chip cookie dough ice cream? So get out there and explore all the wonderful things about your new diet; try all the PLANeTbased foods, and see which ones you love the most. I used to be a pretty conservative eater, but when I start ed chowing down in the name of Mother Earth ("Chowing Down in the Name of Mother Earth" is my new band name), my palate expanded to include all sorts of tastiness that I had no idea even existed. So explore! See what works for you! And then spread the word with other awesome people, because without all of us doing our part, humans are basically dunzo. And I don't want to be responsible for humans being dunzo, because the Earth is pretty much the best and I want my great great great great great grand kids to be around to vote for the first Martian president, Uthuruy Hoombahbahwingdigtoo. (He's gonna do great things for

LOOK!
GOLD!
FOR YOU!

Life is delicious and now you're ready to fully enjoy it. Dig in with a big spoon and eat it all up. I swear, I'm still talking about life here, and not peanut butter chocolate chip cookie dough ice cream. OK, I'm talking about that too. Now it's time to Chow Down in the Name of Mother Earth. (And don't forget to save me some because if you don't, I'll be forced to haunt you from beyond the grave. And I won't be a friendly ghost, either! You should know that by now!)

RIIIGHT... NOW WE'RE FINISHED WITH OUR PLANET PROPAGANDA.

LET'S MOVE ONTO THE TASTY RECIPES...

THIS IS A COOK BOOK AFTER ALL!

JOY.

COMPASSION.

PEACE.

EVERYDAY NACHOS

BUY LOCAL INGREDIENTS FOR AN EVEN LOWER CARBON FOOTPRINT!

FFFRREESSHHH

VEGAN FTW!

PLANET BASED FOOD

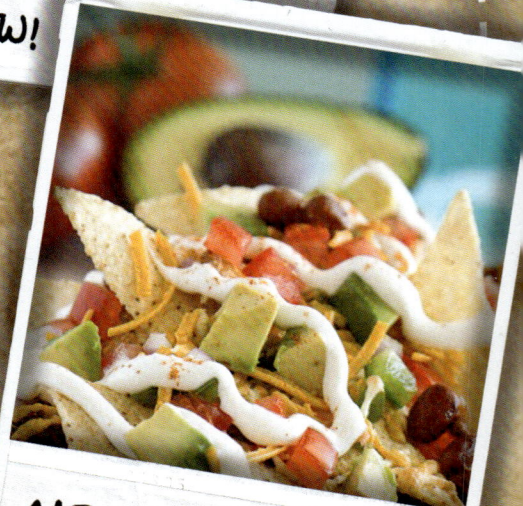

MARRY ME AVOCADO!

EVERYDAY NACHOS
Serves 2
Ingredients:
1 bag of organic corn tortilla chips
1 can of organic vegetarian chili
(or organic vegetarian refried beans)
1 cup shredded Daiya nondairy cheese
1 organic tomato diced
1/2 organic onion diced
1/2 organic bell pepper diced
1 organic avocado diced
1 container of Tofutti Sour Cream
Pinch of salt, pepper, cayenne

Directions:
Preheat your oven to 450 degrees.
On a cookie sheet lay down a layer of tortilla chips. Use 1/2 can of chili to liberally cover the tortilla chips.
Sprinkle 1 cup of shredded Daiya and diced bell pepper over top.
Bake for approx. 10 min.
After baking, sprinkle diced onions, tomatoes and avocado over whole dish.
Drizzle sour cream on top and season to taste with salt, pepper and cayenne.

FINGER GARLICKEN GOOD BREAD.

Garlic bread so good even vampires would eat it.

Ingredients:
8-10 slices of Egg-free sour dough bread.
1/2 cup olive oil.
1-1 1/2 cloves of organic garlic, minced.
Salt, pepper, paprika.

On a large baking sheet, place sliced bread.
Drizzle oil over bread, sprinkle salt, pepper, and paprika and liberally spread minced garlic on all slices.
Broil at high for 25 minutes or until golden. Take extra care not to burn the bread as high broil things go quickly.

FINGER GARLICKEN GOOD BREAD

LETS FACE IT, CHICKS (AND HENS AND ROOSTERS) LOVE VEGANS.

MAKES 4 PATTIES.

INGREDIENTS.
1 CAN OF ORGANIC GARBANZO BEANS
1/2 CUP OF COOKED LONG GRAIN BROWN RICE
1/2 CUP DICED ONION
1/2-1 CUP OF VITAL WHEAT GLUTEN
1 TBS GARLIC POWDER
1 TSP SALT
3 TBS VEGETABLE OIL
RINSE AND STRAIN GARBANZO BEANS

IN A LARGE BOWL, ROUGHLY MASH BEANS WITH THE BACK OF A FORK. MIX IN ONIONS, GARLIC POWDER AND SALT, MIX AND KNEAD IN ENOUGH VITAL WHEAT GLUTEN UNTIL YOU HAVE A FIRM DOUGH. CUT DOUGH INTO 4 EQUAL PIECED, HAND FORM INTO 1/2 INCH THICK BURGER PATTIES AND LET REST FOR 5 MINUTES. IN A LARGE FRYING PAN, ADD 13 TBS OF OIL. HEAT TO MEDIUM/HIGH. WHEN OIL IS HOT, ADD PATTIES TO PAN. PRESS PATTIES WITH THE BACK OF A METAL SPATULA TO EXPEL MOISTURE AND EVENLY COOK PATTIES. FLIP PATTIES WHEN GOLDENING/BROWNING ON BOTTOM AND COOK OTHER SIDE. ADDING MORE OIL MAY BE NECESSARY. ALLOW TO COOL. ENJOY ON BURGER BUNS OR BREAD HEAVILY SPREAD WITH VEGAN MAYO AND ALL YOUR FAVORITE CONDIMENTS.

GET ALL THE CHICKS N BURGER.

Grilled Say Cheese Sandwich

Makes 2 sandwiches

Ingredients:

4 slices of sourdough bread (without eggs)
10 oz. block of Follow Your Heart
"vegan gourmet mozzarella"cheese
1/3 sliced onion
Garlic powder
Salt
Pepper
Just Mayo spread
Organic olive oil

Instructions:

Drizzle oil on the backs of the sliced bread. Flip over and liberally apply Just Mayo spread to each slice (the more the better).

Slice cheese into 1/4" thick slices. Apply cheese to two slices of bread, top with sliced onions.

Sprinkle garlic powder, salt and pepper on top and close sandwiches with remaining slices of bread.

Heat an oiled large frying pan at medium/high heat.

Once hot, lay one sandwich at a time in pan.

Press with the back of metal spatula for 20 seconds.

Cook until underside is golden.

Flip and repeat.

Serve hot.

GRILLED SAY "CHEESE" SANDWICH

HeArtichoke Dip

Ingredients:
1 can organic artichoke hearts,
drained 1/2 cup raw sunflower seeds
1/2 cup water
2 clove organic garlic
1/2 organic white onion, diced
1 teaspoon dijon mustard
2 tsplemon juice
1/4 cup nutritional yeast
2-3 leaves of kale, chopped
1 scallion, diced
salt, pepper

Directions:
Drain artichoke hearts and add to a high powered blender with oil, water, garlic, mustard, lemon juice and yeast. Salt and pepper to taste. Blend to a thick creamy dip.

In pan at medium heat, cook kale and onion in 1/2tbs of oil until onions golden. Lower heat to low/med and pour in dip mix from blender. Warm all the way through. Serve warm with crackers or bread.

ICE-CREAM FOR BREAKFAST!?

SERVES 1-2

INGREDIENTS:
5 FROZEN ORGANIC BANANAS
1/4-3/4 CUP OF PLANT MILK
1-2 TBS OF PEANUT BUTTER/CASHEW
BUTTER/TAHINI
DASH OF CINNAMON

INSTRUCTIONS:
PEAL AND FREEZE 5 OR MORE SUPER
RIPE BANANAS IN A BAG,
THE RIPER THE BETTER!
ONCE FROZEN, CHOP INTO 1/4 INCH SLICES.
ADD BANANAS, CINNAMON AND NUT
BUTTER TO HIGH POWERED
BLENDER OR FOOD PROCESSOR.
ADD JUST ENOUGH MILK TO GET BLENDING
GOING. PULSE BLEND THE MIX TO KEEP IT
AS THICK AS POSSIBLE. FREQUENTLY STOP
AND USE A SPOON OR SPATULA TO MIX
MORE AND THEN PULSE AGAIN.
BLEND UNTIL A THICK CREAMY ICE-CREAM
CONSISTENCY.
SPOON INTO A BOWL AND EAT
IMMEDIATELY.

WHO DOESN'T LOVE ICE-CREAM?

HOW ABOUT HEALTHY ENERGY PACKED ICE-CREAM FOR BREAKFAST?

JUICEY IN THE SKY WITH BLUEBERRIES

Ingredients:
8-10 oz organic orange juice
1 organic banana
1/4 cup blueberries

Instructions:
Blend all ingredients in a high powered blender. Enjoy chilled.

A refreshing energy packed drink

JOY. COMPASSION. PEACE.

Keep the earth spinning, spiral pasta party.

Keep the earth spinning, spiral pasta party

Ingredients.
12oz box of organic wheat/rice spiral pasta
1 can of organic tomato sauce/paste
1 onion sliced or diced
2 cups organic basil
4 - 8 cloves organic garlic minced
1/3 - 1/2 cup olive oil
2 large heads of organic broccoli chopped
1/3 cup nutritional yeast
dash of oregano, salt and black pepper

Instructions:
In a large sauce pan, heat oil at medium/low heat. Add onions and simmer for 3 minutes. Pour and mix in tomato sauce and broccoli. Lower heat to simmer for 8 - 12 minutes, covering may be necessary. Add in garlic, nutritional yeast and basil. Continue to cook until broccoli is desired softness. Cook pasta al dente. Drain pasta and then return pasta to the cooking pot and pour tomato sauce over top, mixing it in. Cook at medium/low heat for an additional 5 minutes at medium/low heat. Serve warm with garlic bread.

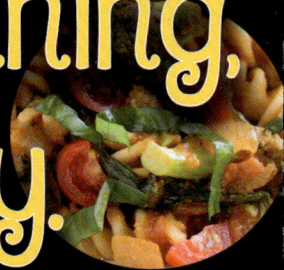

A twist on traditional spiral pasta

Leonardo Da Veggie Burger Masterpiece

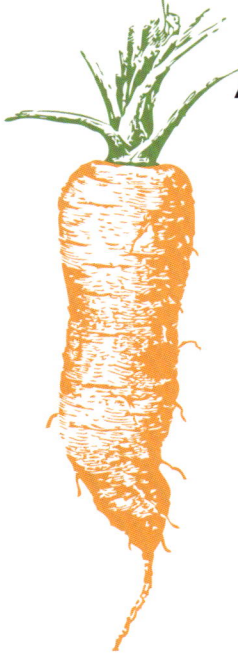

A burger Da Vinci would have enjoyed
(he was vegetarian).
Makes 4 patties.

INGREDIENTS:
1 cup garbanzo beans
1 cup kidney beans
1/3 cup diced onion
1/3 finely shredded beet
1/2-1 cup nutritional yeast
1/4 tsp salt
1/2 tsp garlic powder
dash of pepper

Rinse and thoroughly strain beans. In a large bowl,
mash garbanzo and kidney beans with the back of a fork.
Press/squeeze beets to remove as much juice before adding to
bowl. Mix in onion, beets, yeast, salt, garlic and mix. Add yeast
until mixture is firm enough to hand-form patties. In a frying pan at
medium heat, fry patties until brown on both sides.
Enjoy on a bun with your
favorite condiments.

Leonardo Da Veggie Burger Masterpiece

YOU WILL LOVE ME WHEN YOU'RE HUNGRY!!!

MARK'S BUFFALO WINGS

Ingredients:
12 oz. package of extra-firm tofu
1/3 – 1/2 cup corn starch
1/2 cup buffalo hot sauce (look for a brand that doesn't have palm oil or butter in it)*
1/4 cup of vegan (palm-free) butter
2 tbs canola oil

Directions:
Freeze tofu and then thaw to create a chewy consistency. Thoroughly press and drain tofu block to remove as much water as possible, taking care not to crack of break it apart. The drier the tofu the better.

Cut the tofu block lengthwise into 1" wide fingerlings. Add cornstarch to a bowl and gently but liberally batter tofu. In a medium pan, heat the oil at medium heat and fry tofu until it starts to brown, flip and repeat. Melt the butter and mix in hot sauce, then cover fried tofu in sauce and serve warm with dipping sauce.

OMP OH...MY...PIZZA!

12" SERVES 1-2
MANY GROCERY STORES HAVE PREMADE PIZZA DOUGHS WITHOUT
ANIMAL INGREDIENTS. BUT YOU MAY HAVE A TOUGH TIME FINDING
ORGANIC DOUGHS. SO YOU CAN MAKE YOUR OWN SUPER SIMPLE!

CRUST INGREDIENTS:
.25 OZ PACKAGED ACTIVE DRY YEAST
2 1/2 CUPS OF ORGANIC WHITE FLOUR
1 TEASPOON ORGANIC SUGAR
2 TABLESPOONS ORGANIC OLIVE OIL
1 TEASPOON SALT
1 CUP WARM WATER (110 DEGREES)

TOPPING INGREDIENTS:
1 CUP OF DAIYA MOZZARELLA CHEESE
1/2 CUP OF ORGANIC TOMATO SAUCE
(USE YOUR FAVORITE PASTA SAUCE FOR EXTRA FLAVOR)

ORGANIC VEGETABLES OF CHOICE:
- ONION
- PEPPER
- MUSHROOM
- OLIVES
- BASIL
- SPINACH
- PINEAPPLE
- BROCCOLI
- TOMATO
- VEGGIE SAUSAGE OR PEPPERONI OR CHICKEN ETC.

LET COOL FOR 5 MINUTES BEFORE SERVING

OH...MY...PIZZA!

PIG-LESS PLANT-BASED SALAMI WILL BLOW YOUR MIND!!!

Peaceful Steak and Cheese Sandwich

Peaceful Steak and Cheese Sandwich

Serves 12

Ingredients:
2 Italian style sandwich rolls
10. oz. seitan strips
1/2 organic onion, sliced
1/2 organic green bell pepper, sliced
1 cup shredded Daiya cheese
(mozzarella or cheddar)
1/2 tbs minced organic garlic
1 tbs organic olive oil
1/2 tbs Just Mayo spread
salt and pepper

Instructions:
Slice and open rolls lengthwise. Toast if desired.
Spread thick layer of Just Mayo spread on both
sides of the roll. Add mustard if desired. Heat a
large pan at medium/high heat. Once hot add oil,
onion and bell pepper. Cook until caramelized then
add garlic, salt and pepper. Slice or shred seitan
strips. Add seitan to pan and mix and cook will all
ingredients until seitan is hot all the way through,
about 3 minutes. Lower heat to medium/low and add
1/2 cup of cheese, mix and cook together.
Spoon the meaty cheese mixture onto buns and
serve immediately.

Peanut Butter Cookie Monsieur

PEANUT BUTTER COOKIE MONSIEUR

BUTTER FREE PEANUT BUTTER BAKING PRODUCT.

INGREDIENTS.
1 3/4 CUP ALL PURPOSE PASTRY FLOUR
1/2 A RIPE BANANA
3/4 TSP BAKING SODA
3/4 TSP SALT
1 1/4 CUP ORGANIC SUGAR
3/4 - 1 CUP ORGANIC PEANUT BUTTER (UNSALTED)
1/3 CUP COCONUT BUTTER
3 TABLE SPOONS PLANET MILK

IN A LARGE BOWL, MIX FLOUR, BAKING SODA, AND SALT. IN A SEPARATE BOWL MASH BANANAS WITH THE BACK OF A FORK, MIX IN SUGAR, PEANUT BUTTER, COCONUT BUTTER, MILK. WHISK AS MUCH AS POSSIBLE AND POUR INTO DRY MIX.
PREHEAT OVEN TO 375 DEGREES.
FORM 1 INCH BALLS FROM BATTER AND PLACE ON A UNGREASED BAKING SHEET 2-3 INCHES APART.
BAKE FOR 10 MINUTES OR UNTIL COOKIES BEGIN TO BROWN ON THE EDGES.
LET COOL FOR 5 MINUTES BEFORE REMOVING FROM BAKING SHEET.

Rawlicious Pesto Sauce

Ingredients:

1 1/2 cups of fresh
basil leaves
1/3 cup olive oil
1 cup pine nuts
(or cashews)
5 cloves of garlic
1/3 cup nutritional
yeast
3/4 tsp salt
1/4 tsp pepper

Instructions:

Blend all ingredients in
a food processor until a
creamy paste.
Add more oil or water
to thin.

Rawlicious Pesto Sauce

REAL (TASTY CASHEW) CHEESE

REAL (TASTY CASHEW) CHEESE
1 CUP RAW CASHEWS (SOAKED)
2 CLOVES GARLIC
1 TBS. ORGANIC APPLE CIDER VINEGAR
1/4 CUP WATER
1/4 CUP NUTRITIONAL YEAST
2 TBS. LEMON JUICE
1 TBS. DIJON MUSTARD
SEA SALT AND PEPPER TO TASTE

DIRECTIONS:
SOAK CASHEWS OVERNIGHT IN A BOWL
(MAKES BLENDING EASIER).
ADD ALL INGREDIENTS IN A HIGH POWERED
BLENDER OR FOOD PROCESSOR AND BLEND
UNTIL A THICK CREAMY CONSISTENCY.
SCOOP INTO A CONTAINER WITH A TIGHT
LID AND ALLOW TO CHILL/HARDEN IN THE
REFRIGERATOR FOR A FEW HOURS BEFORE
SERVING. CREATES 1.5 CUPS OF GOODNESS.

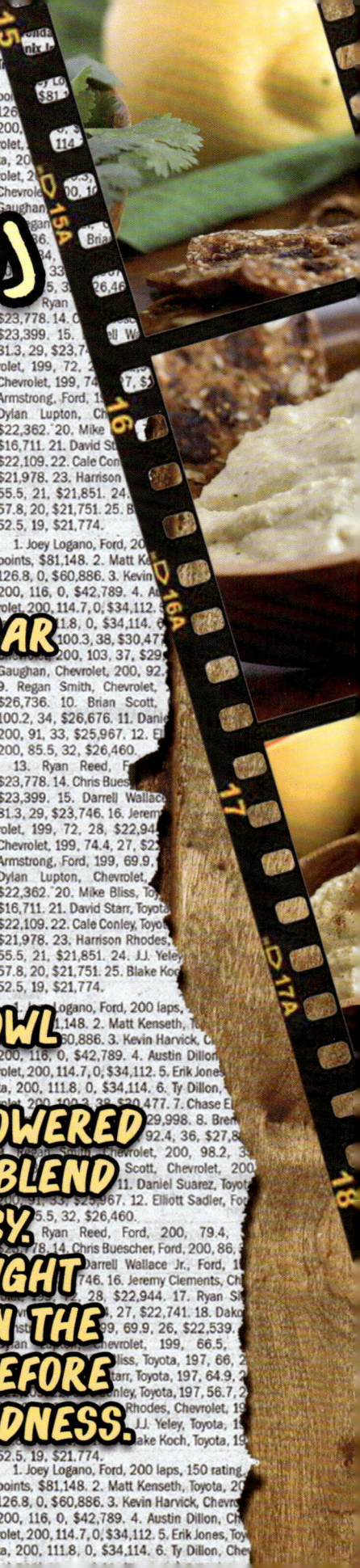

Who doesn't always have left over pasta?

Recycle, Reduce, Reuse Past a Burger

Here are burgers you can make from left over "Keep The Earth Spinning, spiral pasta" recipe. You can also make this from scratch too.

1 cup leftover spiral pasta with tomato sauce cooked in.
1⁄2 cup minced onion.
1⁄2 cup shredded organic beet.
1⁄2-1 cup nutritional yeast
salt and pepper to taste
1 tbs oil

In a large bowl, use the back of a fork to roughly mash pasta, leaving some spirals partially intact.
Press or squeeze shredded beets to remove as much liquid as possible before adding beets to bowl.
Mix in beets, onions, and salt/pepper. Add yeast until mixture is thick enough to hand form patties.
In a frying pan, heat oil at medium/high heat. Add patties to pan and fry evenly on both sides until browning. Enjoy with your favorite condiments on a toasted bun.

Return of the Macaroni and Cheese!

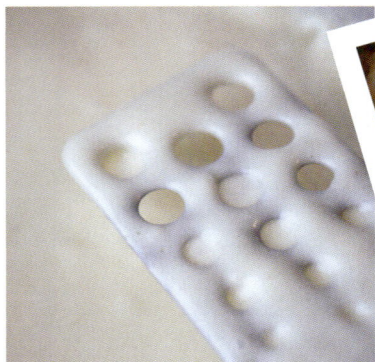

WHO DOESN'T LOVE MAC N CHEESE?

RETURN OF THE MACARONI AND CHEESE!
SERVES 2.

INGREDIENTS:
1/2 LB OF ORGANIC MACARONI PASTA
10 OZ BLOCK OF FOLLOW YOUR HEART "VEGAN GOURMET MOZZARELLA CHEESE"
1/2 CUP OF UNSWEETENED ORGANIC PLANT MILK (SOY, RICE, HEMP, ETC)
2 TABLESPOON ORGANIC OLIVE OIL
PINCH OF BLACK PEPPER
SALT
GARLIC POWDER
OPTIONAL: CAYENNE POWDER

INSTRUCTIONS:
FOLLOW BOX/BAG INSTRUCTIONS FOR PASTA COOKING. COMPLETE PASTA COOKING AND RETURN BACK TO POT/PAN WITH LID BEFORE BEGINNING CHEESE HEATING. CUT CHEESE BLOCK INTO 1/4" CUBES. IN A MEDIUM SAUCEPAN ADD 1 TABLESPOON OF OLIVE OIL FOLLOWED BY CUBED CHEESE. HEAT CHEESE AT MEDIUM/LOW HEAT UNTIL IT BECOMES A THICK LIQUID. WHISK IF NECESSARY. TAKE EXTRA CARE NOT TO OVER HEAT CHEESE. ONCE LIQUID, WHISK IN MILK, REMAINING OIL AND GARLIC POWDER. WHILE THE CHEESE IS STILL HOT, POUR, WHISK, SPATULA AND MIX LIQUID CHEESE INTO MACARONI PASTA, COMPLETELY COVERING PASTA WITH CHEESE. ADD SALT AND PEPPER (AND CAYENNE) TO TASTE. SERVE HOT.

SO JEALOUS CAESAR SALAD

SERVES 2-3

INGREDIENTS:

2-4 HEADS OF ORGANIC ROMAINE LETTUCE

1/2 CUP ORGANIC OLIVE OIL

1/2 CUP ORGANIC SILKEN TOFU

1 TABLESPOON VINEGAR EITHER WHITE OR APPLE CIDER

2 TABLESPOONS ORGANIC LEMON JUICE

2-3 GLOVES OF ORGANIC GARLIC

2 TEASPOONS SALT AND PEPPER

1/2-1 TBS DIJON MUSTARD

OPTIONAL CROUTONS:

2-5 SLICES OF SOURDOUGH BREAD

INSTRUCTIONS:

ROUGHLY CHOP LETTUCE INTO 1" SECTIONS. IN A BLENDER OR FOOD PROCESSOR BLEND OIL, TOFU, VINEGAR, LEMON JUICE, GARLIC, SALT AND MUSTARD TOGETHER. YOU MAY NEED TO ADD A SMALL AMOUNT OF WATER TO THIN DRESSING.

CROUTONS:

CUBE SLICED BREAD, TOSS WITH OIL, SALT AND PEPPER. BAKE ON A COOKIE SHEET AT 350 DEGREES FOR 3-7 MINUTES OR UNTIL SLIGHTLY CRISPY.

TOSS CHOPPED LETTUCE WITH DRESSING AND CROUTONS. SERVE CHILLED OR ROOM TEMP.

Southern Fried Summer Time.

INGREDIENTS:
1 CUP VITAL WHEAT GLUTEN
3/4 - 1 CUP WARM WATER
8 CUPS OF BULLION/VEGETABLE BROTH WATER
2-4 CUPS ALL PURPOSE FLOUR.
4-8 CUPS VEGETABLE OIL (PEANUT OIL WORKS BEST)
1 TSP TURMERIC POWDER
1 TBS GARLIC POWDER
1 TBS ONION POWDER
1 TSP CAYENNE POWDER
2-4 TSP SALT
DASH OF BLACK PEPPER
1 PACKET OF RAPID RISING YEAST.

IN A LARGE BOWL MIX WHEAT GLUTEN, 1 TSP TURMERIC, 1/2 TBS GARLIC POWDER, 1/2 TBS ONION POWDER, 1 TSP SALT AND PACKET OF YEAST TOGETHER. SLOWLY ADD WARM WATER AND STIR INTO DRY MIX. KNEAD AS NEEDED. LET DOUGH REST FOR 5 MINUTES. IN A LARGE POT, SIMMER 8 CUPS OF VEGETABLE BROTH. TEAR DOUGH INTO STRIPS. THE MORE YOU PULL THE DOUGH APART THE BETTER FOR TEXTURE. BOIL/SIMMER DOUGH FOR 20 MINUTES.

IN A LARGE BOWL/DISH MIX ALL PURPOSE FLOUR, 1/2 TBS GARLIC POWDER, 1/2 TBS ONION POWDER, 1 TSP CAYENNE POWDER, 13 TSP SALT.

WARM OIL IN A FRIER OF DEEP POT AT MEDIUM/HIGH.

DRAIN DOUGH FROM BROTH. BATTER DOUGH IN DRY MIX AND FRY IN OIL UNTIL GOLDEN BROWN ON BOTH SIDES. STRAIN AND ENJOY.

INSTEAD OF FRYING THE PLANET WITH GLOBAL WARMING, FRY UP SOME PLANET-BASED SOUTHERN CHICKN.

Stir it UP!

Stir fry for the planet.

Stir it UP!

Serves 2-4

Ingredients:

2 cups brown rice
Large head of organic broccoli chopped
2-4 small bok choy heads chopped
1 small/medium sweet onion sliced
3-5 cups of chopped kale
3-5 cups of chopped rainbow chard, with stems 25 cloves of minced garlic
5-10 white button mushrooms sliced
1/2 bell pepper sliced
1-2 tbs soy sauce
1/2 tbs vegetable oil
1 cup warm water
Salt and pepper to taste

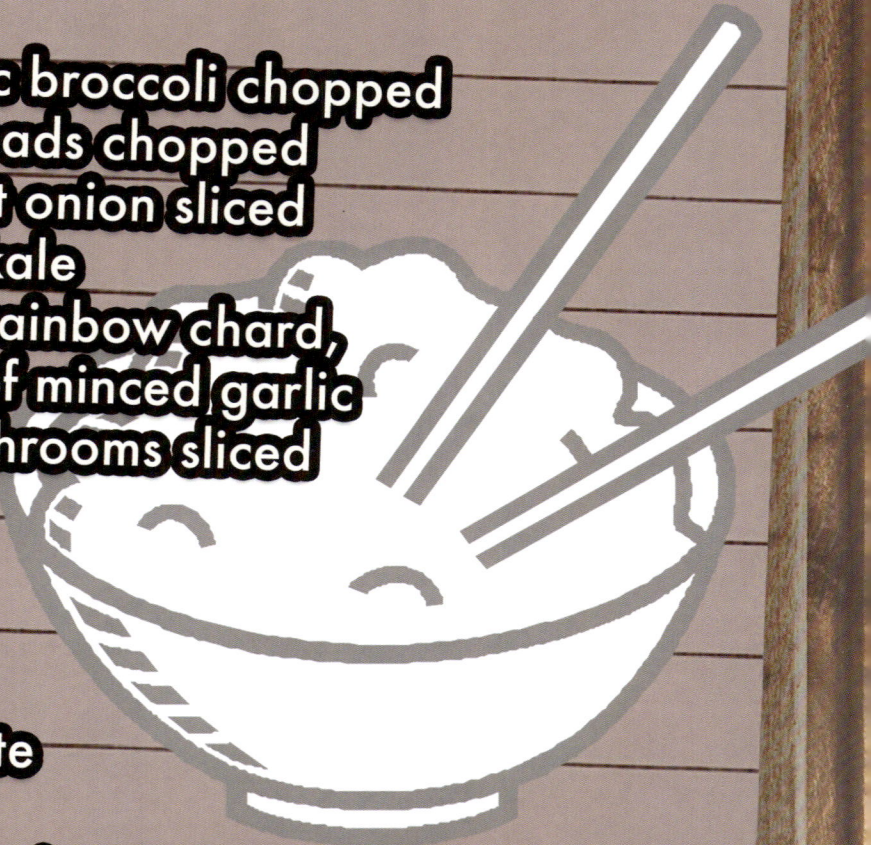

Make the rice following instructions.
In a large deep pan or frying wok with lid, add oil at medium heat. When the oil is warm add sliced onion and bell pepper. Allow to simmer for 1 minute to absorb oil. Add broccoli and garlic, carefully add 1/2 cup of warm water, cover and let simmer for 2-4 minutes. Uncover and add remaining ingredients. Add water if needed, stir and cover again for 2 minutes. Uncover and stir as needed to cook vegetables evenly. Enjoy over brown rice.

SUE ME, OR SUSHI?

SUE ME, OR SUSHI?
STAY OUT OF TROUBLE AND KEEP FISH IN THE OCEAN WITH PLANET-BASED SUSHI

INGREDIENTS:

4 CUPS OF COOKED ORGANIC SHORT GRAIN RICE (WHITE OR BROWN) 1 TBS RICE VINEGAR

1/2 TBS ORGANIC SUGAR

1-2 ORGANIC AVOCADO

1 LARGE ORGANIC CARROT

1 ORGANIC CUCUMBER

1/2 ORGANIC ONION

4 SHEETS OF ORGANIC NORI

MIX SUGAR AND VINEGAR TOGETHER. STIR IN VINEGAR MIX INTO COOKED RICE. ALLOW RICE TO SIT AND COOL TO ROOM TEMPERATURE.

SLICE AVOCADO INTO THICK SLICES. SLICE CUCUMBER INTO LONG 1 4 INCH WIDE SLICES. SLICE CARROTS AND ONION INTO ULTRA THIN LONG SLICES.

ON A BAMBOO SUSHI ROLLER, LAY ONE SHEET OF NORI SHINNY SIDE DOWN.

ADD 1 CUP OF RICE TO THE NORI SHEET AND EVENLY SPREAD IT OVER 7/8 TH OF THE NORI, LEAVING A 1 INCH STRIP ALONG THE SIDE FURTHEST FROM YOU.

LAY YOUR SLICED INGREDIENTS IN A STRIP ON THE FIRST THIRD OF THE NORI SHEET.

USING YOUR FINGERS TO HOLD THE NORI AGAINST THE BAMBOO ROLLER, BEGIN TO ROLL THE NORI OVER ITSELF WITH YOUR THUMBS ON THE UNDERSIDE OF THE ROLLER.

PULL THE ROLLER BACK AND CONTINUE TO ROLL THE SUSHI PRESSING FIRMLY ALL ALONG THE WAY. CUT THE LONG ROLL INTO DESIRED LENGTHS AND ENJOY WITH SOY SAUCE, WASABI AND SLICED GINGER.

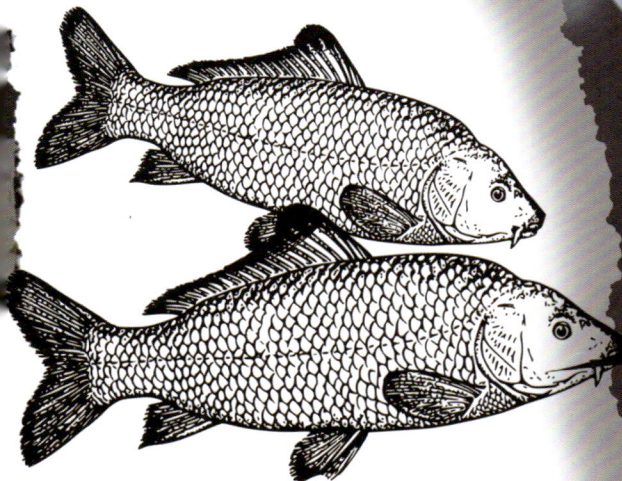

I'm glad nothing fishy is going on here

SUPERHERO SMOOTHIES

SuperHero Smoothies
A powerful smoothie to save the earth with!

2 organic bananas
1/2 cup frozen organic strawberries
1/2 cup frozen organic blueberries
1/2 cup soaked cashews
1 tbs of organic blue green algae
1 cup organic kale shredded
1/2 - 1 cup organic coconut milk

Directions: In a high powered blender, blend a 1/2 cup of milk, cashews and kale until liquified. Add in frozen berries and blend further, followed by bananas and algae and remaining milk to desired consistency.
Enjoy immediately.

TempHaaaay! Reuben

TEMPHAAAAY! REUBEN
SERVES 2 - 4

INGREDIENTS:
TEMPEH STRIPS 8 OZ.
SMALL ORGANIC ONION SLICED
4 CLOVES OF ORGANIC GARLIC MINCED
1/4 CUP OF ORGANIC BALSAMIC VINEGAR
2 TBS ORGANIC OLIVE OIL
2 TBS SOY SAUCE OR BRAGGS
8 SLICES OF ORGANIC RYE BREAD
2 CUPS OF ORGANIC SAUERKRAUT
MONTEREY JACK VEGAN CHEESE (10 OZ)
THINLY SLICED
1/4 CUP VEGAN MAYO
3 TBS RELISH
2 TSP KETCHUP

DIRECTIONS:
THERE ARE A HOST OF MARINATED TEMPEH STRIPS ALREADY
AVAILABLE, BUT IF YOU CAN'T FIND ANY OR JUST WANT TO
DO YOUR OWN OR ADD FLAVOR, FOLLOW THESE INSTRUCTIONS.
ADD OIL TO A MEDIUM/LARGE FRYING PAN AT LOW/MED HEAT.
ONCE HOT, ADD ONION, GARLIC, TEMPEH, VINEGAR, SOY
SAUCE. MIX THOROUGHLY TOGETHER AND ALLOW TO MARINATE
FOR 15-20MIN AT LOW/MED HEAT. IN A SMALL BOWL MIX MAYO
AND KETCHUP TOGETHER. ONCE IT'S NICE AND PINK, MIX IN
RELISH. LIBERALLY APPLY THE SPREAD TO EACH SLICE OF
BREAD AND COVER WITH SLICED CHEESE. ADD MARINATED
TEMPEH AND ONIONS TO HALF OF THE BREAD, COVER WITH
SAUERKRAUT AND CLOSE SANDWICH WITH REMAINING
SLICES OF DRESSED SLICES. IN A SLIGHTLY OILED PAN, TOAST
UNTIL BREAD GOLDENS OR CHEESE MELTS. ENJOY WARM!

TOO GOOD TO BE TUNAH SALAD

SAVING FISH AND EATING GREAT!

INGREDIENTS:
1 CAN OF ORGANIC GARBANZO BEANS
1/2 CUP ORGANIC WALNUTS MINCED
4 ORGANIC CELERY STICKS MINCED
1-2 TBS OF JUST MAYO/VEGAN MAYO
1-4 TSP SALT
DASH OF PEPPER
1-2 TSP DILL
1-2 TSP KELP FLAKES/GRANULES OR FINELY SHREDDED/MINCED NORI

DIRECTIONS:
RINSE AND DRAIN GARBANZO BEANS FROM THE CAN. IN A MEDIUM SIZE BOWL, MASH BEANS WITH THE BACK OF A FORK. ADD MAYO, SALT, DILL, CELERY, WALNUTS, KELP AND PEPPER AND MIX TOGETHER. SERVE WITH SLICED BREAD OR CRACKERS.

TOFURIFFIC SCRAMBLE

Tofuriffic Scramble
Serves 2

Ingredients:
12oz extra firm tofu
1/2-1 organic red onion, sliced or diced
1/2 organic red bell pepper, sliced or diced
1/2 organic green bell pepper, sliced or diced

Sauce:
1/4 cup organic olive oil
1/2 tsp organic garlic powder 1/2 tsp salt
1/4 tsp cumin
1/4 tsp turmeric
1/4 tsp chili powder
1/4 tsp pepper
Optional 1 TB Just Mayo

Instructions:
Drain tofu from container. With the backside of a fork break up firm tofu into 1-1/2 irregular crumbles. Blend sauce ingredients in a blender or food processor with enough warm water to make a pourable liquid. In a large oiled frying pan, add tofu, onion, and peppers. Briefly saute before pouring in sauce. Saute ingredients at medium/high heat until tofu just begins to become crisp on the edges. Serve warm with ketchup, salsa, cilantro or toast.

Berry Good French Toast

Berry Good French Toast
Serves 2-4

Ingredients:
5-7 thick slices of Italian bread (most traditional Italian bread only has water, salt, flour, yeast and a sweetener to help rising)
6 oz. soy or coconut vanilla yogurt
1/2-2 cups of plant milk (soy, hemp, rice)
1/2-1 tbs cinnamon
1 tsp vanilla extract
1/2 tsp salt
2 tbs coconut oil (solid)

Instructions:
Blend yogurt, cinnamon, vanilla and salt with enough milk to thin down to a thick creamy liquid.
Pour into a large bowl or baking pan.
Heat a large skillet or frying pan at medium/high heat with 1/2 tbs of coconut oil. Soak sliced bread for 30 seconds. Avoid making the bread soggy.
Fry bread in skillet for 35 minutes or until browning, flip and repeat. Serve with organic maple syrup or agave nectar.

Where's Waffle?!

WE'VE ALL LOOKED FOR WALDO, BUT LOOK NO FURTHER FOR WAFFLES!

INGREDIENTS:

3/4 CUPS ORGANIC APPLE SAUCE
6 TBS ORGANIC CANOLA OIL OR MELTED COCONUT OIL
1/2 CUP WATER
1 1/2 CUP PLANT MILK
1 3/4 CUP UNBLEACHED ALL PURPOSE FLOUR
1 TBS BAKING POWDER
1 TBS GRANULATED ORGANIC SUGAR OR AGAVE NECTAR
PINCH OF SALT

DIRECTIONS:
IN A BLENDER MIX APPLE SAUCE, OIL, WATER, MILK AND SUGAR TOGETHER. IN A LARGE BOWL MIX FLOUR, BAKING POWDER AND SALT. CREATE A DEPRESSION IN THE MIDDLE AND WHISK IN LIQUID MIXTURE. SCOOP A 1/2 CUP OF BATTER INTO YOUR FAVORITE WAFFLE IRON AT A TIME. IF WAFFLES ARE STICKING TOO MUCH ADD A BIT MORE OIL. ENJOY WARM WITH PALM-FREE VEGAN BUTTER/COCONUT OIL AND AGAVE NECTAR.

World's Happiest Milk.

Ingredients:

1 cup soaked hemp seeds

4 - 8 cups coconut water

1 tbs agave nectar (optional)

1 tsp salt (optional)

Instructions:

Soak hemp seeds overnight in water. Drain seeds and add all ingredients to a high powered blender. Add in more or less coconut water to thin or thicken to desired consistency. Store in a glass mason jar with a tight lid. Store refrigerated and consume within 5 days. Shake before drinking.

World's Happiest Milk

Hemp seeds are a superfood! It's the happiest milk because it has a lower environmental footprint, but it won't get you high.

YOU MAY CREAMY PENNE PASTA IN YOUR PANTS IT TASTES SO GOOD

SERVES 2-4

INGREDIENTS:

1/2 LB OF ORGANIC PENNE PASTA
2 CUPS ORGANIC CASHEWS
2-4 CUPS OF VEGETABLE BROTH
8 CLOVES OF ORGANIC GARLIC, SLICED, 1/2 CUP ORGANIC OLIVE OIL
1 ORGANIC AVOCADO, SLICED
2 ORGANIC SCALLIONS, DICED
1/4-1/2 ORGANIC RED BELL PEPPER, DICED
SALT, PEPPER

INSTRUCTIONS:

PREPARE PASTA ACCORDING TO BOX, KEEP WARM.

IN A SAUCEPAN, SIMMER GARLIC AND BELL PEPPER IN OIL UNTIL GARLIC BEGINS TO GOLDEN.

IN A HIGH POWERED BLENDER OR FOOD PROCESSOR, BLEND CASHEWS WITH ENOUGH VEGETABLE BROTH TO BRING THE CASHEWS TO A CREAMY LIQUID. BLEND IN SIMMERED OIL AND GARLIC, EXCLUDE THE BELL PEPPER. SALT AND PEPPER TO TASTE. TOSS PASTA WITH CREAMY SAUCE. SERVE WARM TOPPED WITH DICED SCALLIONS AND SLICED AVOCADO.

You May Creamy Penne Pasta in your pants it tastes so good.